Born in 1921 in Stockholm, Sweden, Krister Stendahl grew up to become not only a priest and a scholar but a leader and a champion of movements seeking greater equality, justice, and inclusion in the academy, the church, and the world. He was ordained to the ministry in the Church of Sweden in 1944 and served as curate in a country parish before returning to the University of Uppsala. There he served as chaplain to students as he also pursued graduate studies in New Testament and contributed to the international student movement. On receiving his doctorate in 1954, he accepted an invitation to join the faculty at Harvard Divinity School, where he would teach for the next thirty years, serving also as Dean of that school during the turbulent late 1960s and 1970s. In 1984 Stendahl returned to Sweden to serve as Bishop of Stockholm, and the four years of his tenure were noted for the gifts of leadership and public witness he brought to the office. On retirement he returned to the United States, serving as a chaplain at the Divinity School and then as professor of Christian Studies at Brandeis University. His many contributions to Pauline studies, to ecumenical and interfaith dialogue, to the recognition of women and of sexual minorities in the church, as well as mentoring countless students, are more remarkable for the physical limitation and pain of the rheumatoid disease that struck him already at the age of sixteen and caused the church to hesitate about ordaining him. Stendahl died in April of 2008. He is survived by his wife, Brita, three children, eight grandchildren, and three great-grandchildren.

Final Account
Paul's Letter to the Romans

Krister Stendahl

Foreword by Jaroslav Pelikan

Fortress Press
Minneapolis

FINAL ACCOUNT
Paul's Letter to the Romans

First Fortress Press edition 1995. First published in 1993 by University Lutheran Church, Cambridge, Massachusetts.

Library of Congress Cataloging-in-Publication Data
Stendahl, Krister.
[Final account, or, Paul's letter to the Romans]
Final account: Paul's letter to the Romans / Krister Stendahl;
foreword by Jaroslav Pelikan.—1st Fortress Press ed.
p. cm.
Originally published: Final account, or, Paul's letter to the Romans.
Cambridge, Mass.: University Lutheran Church, © 1993.
ISBN 978-0-8006-2922-9 (alk. paper)
1. Bible. N.T. Romans—Criticism, interpretation, etc.
I. Title. II. Title: Paul's letter to the Romans.
BS2665.2.S83 1995 227'.107—dc20

The paper used in this publication meets the minimum requirements of American National Standard for Information Sciences—Permanence of Paper for Printed Library Materials, ANSI Z329.48-1984.
Manufactured in the U.S.A.

Contents

Foreword
Jaroslav Pelikan

As Krister Stendahl says in the preface to this slender but potent volume, we have been friends for over four decades, sometimes seeing each other quite often and sometimes not for years, but always being able to pick up the conversation almost at midsentence, even though he was at Harvard and I at Yale.

Repeatedly, that conversation dealt with the themes that sound and resound here—the relation of the two Testaments, the counterpoint between Scripture and Tradition, the creative tensions between scholarship and proclamation, and, over and over, the burden and the glory of being heirs of the Lutheran Reformation. That last theme recurs on these pages with almost Wagnerian regularity, with that combination of self-deprecation and self-confidence at which Krister Stendahl is such a master. Holding all these themes together, for reasons that lie in our common history as well as in the special perspective of each of us, is the haunting problem of Israel and the Church. It is a problem that haunts both of us, as it haunted Paul—and as it ought to haunt the Church. And its meaning is wrapped up with the definition of Paul's apostolic mission, and therefore with the interpretation of the Epistle to the Romans.

About two-thirds of the way through the book (page 35), this epigram suddenly looms into view: "In the very text that comes to us through tradition lies the very truth that criticizes that tradition." I would, I suppose, tend to put it in a converse fashion: "The only reason reformers can pit the text of Scripture against Tradition is that the Tradition has preserved it." Either way, it sets forth an axiom for which the Epistle to the Romans is one of the most fascinating of case studies (the Sermon on the Mount being another). As an earlier capsule history of interpretation puts it (page 10), "Lutheran tradition just knows that the purpose of Romans is to teach justification by faith without the works of the law. Calvinists just know that it is the chief text from which to get the proper doctrine of predestination, and Catholic tradition takes the second chapter as its chief text for substantiating its glorious and correct doctrine of natural law. Augustine, by mistranslating, found the doctrine of original sin in chapter five." Indeed, it was a text from Romans that Augustine was admonished to "take and read" at his conversion, a text from Romans that Luther was struggling to understand when he had his "tower experience," Romans as summarized in Luther's preface that caused Wesley's heart at Aldersgate to be "strangely warmed," and a commentary on Romans that became, in the hands of Karl Barth, " a bombshell thrown into the playground of the theologians."

Now unless I am prepared, with some scholars, to suppose that no one has understood the New Testament until I came along, this range of encounters with the Epistle to the Romans must prompt the question: How has it been possible for one document to have had such a spectrum of effects, each of which has been able to lay claim to something in the epistle? And what has been the relation between each of these interpretations and the situation—or, if you insist, the *Sitz im Leben*—of the interpreter and of the interpreter's church (if any)? Krister Stendahl, as scholar and as preacher, as dean and as bishop, has demonstrated a remarkable capacity simultaneously to resonate to tradition and to be critical toward it. This capacity has included a musicality for a tradition to which his (and my) tradition has been largely tonedeaf, such as the rabbinical, as well as for a tradition that is close to my roots but not to his, such as the Eastern Orthodox (implicit in several places even here). Therefore he embodies the very quality to which he points: that by the tradition which he has transmitted he has equipped all of us who learn from him to go beyond him. And that, too, is a fitting position for someone who does not want to make disciples but to be one.

I am honored and delighted to salute a cherished colleague and beloved friend and to thank him here for yet another precious gift.

Preface

Romans is Paul's final account of his theology of mission. It is not a theological tractate on justification by faith. It is not a pastoral letter dealing with the specific problems in Rome, as the Corinthian correspondence is with respect to Corinth. Romans 15 makes clear that Paul felt he had no authority to interfere with life in the Roman churches. But he was anxious that they have a clear understanding of his apostolic mission as he planned to leave the East and go West to Spain. Thus Romans is Paul's account of how his mission to the Gentiles was grounded not only in his call to be Apostle to the Gentiles but also in Scripture, the only Scripture the first Christians had, that is, the Old Testament. Or perhaps we should say the First Testament.

Romans is Paul's account of how his mission to the Gentiles fit into God's total mission to the world, the *tikkun*, the mending of the creation (cf. Roman 8:18–25), and hence particularly the redemption of Israel. When I speak of Romans as the account of Paul's theology of mission, I am convinced that Pauline theology has its organizing center in Paul's apostolic perception of his mission to the Gentiles. Consequently, Romans is central to our understanding of Paul, not because of its doctrine of justification, but because the doctrine of justification is here in its original and authentic setting: as an argument for the status of Paul's Gentile converts on the model of Abraham (Romans 4).

Although not intended by Paul to be "final," this account of his mission became so. The journey with the offering of the Gentile churches to the church in Jerusalem seems to have led to his arrest. He came to Rome not as a free man on his way to Spain but as a prisoner, and in Rome he was executed. There were further letters written under his name and authority, in the manner acceptable in those days. But the Epistle to the Romans remains the final account by Paul. It is important that when we read it we get it right.

I have pondered how to do that for more than forty years. I never managed to write the commentary of my dreams. When I tried, I was too overwhelmed. What you find here are some notes and musings rescued from tapes by Missy Daniel. She has prepared this edition, together with Brita Stendahl.

Four of the five lectures that roam selectively through Romans were given in the summer (winter) of 1982 in Perth, Australia, at the Australasian Theological Conference of the Australia and New Zealand Theological Society. That proved to be important to me, since it was there I learned to give the doctrine of the Trinity serious reconsideration. The lecture series parallel to mine, by Professor Dietrich Ritschl, now of Heidelberg, opened my eyes, and my understanding of God has been much enriched ever since—to imagine "God beyond our imaging and imagining, a mystery that is not in the image of splendid isolation but eternal being in mutual interrelationship, organic, cosmic, life-giving energy, creative and transcendent," as I wrote in 1990 in *Energy for Life,* a small book for the World Council of Churches. As a matter of fact, each of my three visits to Australia has engendered new insights into how to speak about God, to God, and for God, and how to shut up before God. Many grateful thoughts wander, no fly back to Australia.

The first chapter in this volume, on Paul and Israel, is transcribed from my lecture in December 1991 at Brandeis University when I was inaugurated as the first Kraft-Hiatt Professor in Christian Studies. I am grateful for having it included. My thinking about Romans 11 has changed over the years. In the Preface to *Paul among Jews and Gentiles* (Fortress Press, 1976), I had reason to note how I had moved away from Johannes Munck's view (*Paul and the Salvation of Mankind,* 1959). He saw the mission to the Gentiles as just a vehicle toward the salvation of Israel. I found that view to be a "tour de force" (p. vi). The way I then expressed my thinking about Romans 11 has repeatedly been referred to as representing a two-covenant model, or two ways of salvation, one for Jews and one for Gentiles. In re-reading pages 3–5 of *Paul among Jews and Gentiles*—the pages referred to by those who bother with such precision—I can see how readers could get that impression, especially so because I noted the similarities with the thoughts of Franz Rosenzweig (*Star of Redemption*). I should have spelled out how and why I felt—and now more clearly see—the two-covenant model to be an expression of "misplaced concreteness." As in 1974 so now in the lecture "Paul and Israel" from 1991, my point is the *mystery* by which "the mission urge to convert Israel is held in check"

(*Paul among Jews and Gentiles*, p. 4). To say more is to say too much. To say less is to miss Paul's insight.

There is much to apologize for on my part in these notes and musings on Romans. My speaking style is so different from my writing style. That is no doubt one reason why it is so difficult for me to transform a transcribed tape into a proper chapter of a book. I have tried many times and have failed. So others have been kind enough to help me. Emilie T. Sander did so with the tapes that became *Paul among Jews and Gentiles*, lectures from the early 1960s published in 1976 by Fortress Press. Now Missy Daniel and Brita Stendahl have come to my aid and have allowed the spoken style to prevail, warts and all. It would be arrogant to compare myself with Paul, but there is a slight analogy in his final recognition of his inability to do all that he wanted to do or even what he thought God wanted him to do. Thus my gratitude to Missy and Brita, for their labor of love is great indeed.

Most of the references to the text are my rather free translations and paraphrases. The complete text of Romans reprinted here is the Revised Standard Version, which I still consider to be the most useful translation for study purposes, because it has an adequate closeness to the Greek. I hold that view together with the conviction that translations like the New Revised Standard Version and the *Lectionary for the Christian People* (Fortress Press and Pueblo, 1987–1988) are preferable for liturgical readings—and perhaps the King James Version on the High Holy Days.

Needless to say, the reader will find some repetitions, not least in the treatment of Romans 9–11, both in the lecture on Paul and Israel and in the sequential notes on the Epistle in the Australian lectures. But I hope there is enough difference in perspective to make repetition a positive phenomenon.

Finally, it is an honor to have Jaroslav Pelikan write a Foreword to this book. It brings back strong memories of my first meeting with him in the winter of 1952 in St. Louis. I have often spoken about his lecture on the Augsburg Confession at the then honorable Concordia Seminary as one of my theological and intellectual "Aha!" experiences. What a feast it was!

Around that time I had also begun to see and feel the gap between Paul's thinking about Jews and Gentiles and the introspective Lutheran interpretation that I had learned from my teachers. These thoughts came over me when I was a chaplain listening to student confessions in the sacristy of Uppsala Cathedral. The preoccupation with sin and forgiveness somehow did not square with Paul who, according to his authentic epistles, does not ever use the word "forgiveness." However much one stressed forgiveness of sins, it seemed to chain the mind and life of serious Christians to the self-centered cycle of their sins needing forgiveness. Paul thought otherwise.

Hence my constant return to him and to the very Epistle on which the Lutheran tradition came to base its preoccupation. Jary will have his say, for he knows Luther and the Lutheran tradition, as I claim to know Paul. Our meeting in this book is remarkable.

This small book was originally produced in order to raise funds for University Lutheran Church in Cambridge, Massachusetts, the church that has nurtured our family from the time of our arrival in the United States in 1954. It was printed in one hundred copies, duly numbered and signed, and offered to alumnae/i, members, and friends of the congregation in recognition of major generosity. Now all the copies are gone. As the book was a gift to University Lutheran Church, that church holds the contract with Fortress Press, and to it go the royalties. Thus I can without shame hope for many readers.

1
Paul and Israel

Two problems bothered Paul theologically. What troubled him was not sin, nor his conscience, as I have tried to show in some of my earlier writings. And the problem was really not the law, either in the sense of Torah or in the sense of *nomos.* But two things did bother Paul theologically and existentially.

The first problem was Paul himself. Knowing his importance as the apostle to the Gentiles, it troubled him no end that God did not see fit to keep him healthy and able to function at all times. Paul seems to have had a serious physical handicap (my unprovable guess is that he was an epileptic), and he did not think that was good planning on God's part, since he was so important, and time was so short.

The second problem that worried Paul deeply was Israel. How could it be that, while his mission to the Gentiles on the specific orders of Messiah grew spectacularly, Israel itself did not respond? The coming in of the Gentiles by means of Paul's mission did not seem to strike Israel as a strong sign of the *eschaton,* the restoration of the coming age, as Paul had been taught in synagogue. It worried him. Hence the title of this chapter, "Paul and Israel."

Paul could not rest his theological mind until he found a satisfactory answer to these two questions. They might not be the questions that have struck the Christian tradition as the most troublesome, but one sign of great theologians is that they see problems where others see no problems, and they see right through the problems that are obstacles for others. Paul had to come to grips with what he saw as real problems.

It was difficult to be sick within the life-affirming early Christian community. When writing to the Christians in Galatia Paul remarked, "You were wonderful because you believed my word, although I was stranded among you due to sickness" (Gal. 4:13f). When he got angry with the Corinthians he could hurl at them the observation, "Since you misbehave at your meetings, some of you are sick and some have even died" (1 Cor. 11:30). A sick apostle was not a good advertisement for the cause. This was especially painful in Corinth, where Paul came up against the "sunshine" apostles (2 Cor. 11:5 and 12:11) and missionaries who had weighty letters of recommendation about their powers of health and healing (2 Cor. 3:1). It bothered him that they could describe him as pitiful in appearance, even though they had to admit that he sounded strong when he wrote from a distance (2 Cor. 10:10).

Furthermore, Paul's frequent references to delays or changes in his itinerary may partly witness to his being incapacitated. His different perceptions of the cause of his changes in travel plans is revealing. What Paul saw as Satan's interference in 1 Thess. 2:18 (cf. 2 Cor. 12:7) is seen in the Book of Acts as guidance by "the Spirit of Jesus."

Three times Paul had gone into the wilderness to have it out with the Lord, who had asked him to do this job. After the third of these Christ-wrestling retreats, he finally learned, "When I am weak God's power shines through a little better" (2 Cor. 12:10). Or, as he says in another note to the Corinthians, "This treasure I have in pots of clay so that the overwhelming power comes from God and not from me" (2 Cor. 4:7).

Paul made peace with his weakness. It had nothing to do with sin; that association was introduced later to the Christian tradition, and it came not least of all through Augustine. Paul's weakness was something that had hit him from without. He felt it as a thorn stuck in his flesh, an angel of Satan slapping him in the face (2 Cor. 12:7). He learned to accept it as God's way of making him a theologian of the cross.

But what about Israel? By and large Israel seemed to say no to the Gospel about Jesus as the Messiah. It did not seem to respond as nicely as Luke had Simeon, the old man in the Temple, respond when he took the baby Jesus in his arms and sang, "For mine eyes have seen thy salvation which thou hast prepared before the face of all people, a light to lighten the Gentiles, and the glory of thy people Israel" (Luke 2:30f.). On the whole, Israel's answer seemed to be a stubborn no, and how was Paul going to come to grips with that?

Paul thought of himself as an apostle to the Gentiles; therein lies his whole identity as we know it from his writings. That is the starting point. That is where everybody must begin when trying to understand the Pauline phenomenon. Paul did not understand himself as a convert from one religion to another. That interpretation is both anachronistic and alien to Paul's perception. He described his own call in the same categories with which the prophet Jeremiah spoke about his; humility was not Paul's greatest asset.

Paul was arrogant. But he was so blatantly arrogant that one can somehow cope with it. He was always the greatest: the greatest of sinners, the greatest of apostles, the greatest when it came to speaking in tongues, the greatest at having been persecuted. That is because he wasn't married. Or perhaps that is *why* he wasn't married. Nobody could stand him—but he was great, and that makes his battle with his weakness so moving on a quite personal level. The Messiah, Jesus Christ, chose this apostle for a specific task, and therefore all his writings are expressions of his ministry, not diaries or journal notes about his inner struggles. There is no private Paul who falls in love with Christ so deeply that he even feels called to the ministry. Paul was a Jew, hand-picked to be the apostle of Jesus Christ to the Gentiles.

Paul was not coming from defeats. There is no reason to believe that he had difficulties with his Jewish tradition or with the Torah. On the contrary, he describes himself, with usual humility: "When it comes to obeying the commandments, I was blameless" (Phil. 3:6).

One of the most interesting examples in this regard is found in the seventh chapter of Paul's epistle to the Romans (though perhaps the text is most often used to make the opposite point). In that chapter our contemporary society, interested in if not crazed by psychology, finds the beloved words, "I cannot understand that I act as I act. The good things I want to do I do not, and the bad things I do not want to do I do."

How does the passage continue? I always ask that question in lectures and classes, and I always get the answer I expect, which is the wrong one. Many people think that Paul goes on to say, "Wretched person that I am, who is going to deliver me from this body of sin?" But that is not what Paul himself got out of the distinction between what one wants to do and what one actually often ends up doing. How did Paul put it? He said, "Now if it is that way, then I agree with the law that it is good." And he went on, "I delight in the law of God."

The distinction proves the goodness of the law. Paul did not fall down in spirals of anguish. He proudly affirmed that since we know the difference between what we want to do and what we do not actually do, our true egos are on God's side: "So I, with my true ego, serve the law of God." This is not the point one usually gets out of this "psychological" passage. Paul was simply saying that the law is not at fault; the fault lies with the limitations of the human condition. Paul was speaking not about the body of sin, but about the body of death. We are all to die.

Paul's problems were of many kinds, and his different epistles speak about various ones. The concept most strongly identified with him in the Western tradition after Augustine is what Augustine called justification by faith, justification without the works of the law. In the Lutheran Reformation this concept came to the rescue of the plagued conscience. We need only look at Albrecht Dürer's art, where even the images of living human beings look like skeletons, to feel what enormous weight life and death levied on the culture. The problem of concentrating on the human conscience, which had started with Augustine, got its theological explosion in Luther—and perhaps its psychological explosion in Sigmund Freud—and has played a large role of the Western spiritual tradition.

But Paul's notion of justification by faith did not come as an answer to the question, how can I find a gracious God? Paul only mentioned justification by faith when he discussed the status of his Gentile converts. Speaking about justification by faith was, instead, his way of defending the right of the Gentiles to be included in the consummation and redemption now underway—by faith. Here Paul had made an exegetical find. He discovered that in Genesis 15, "Abraham believed and it was counted him unto righteousness." But not until Genesis 17 was there any word about circumcision. What a discovery this was for Paul! With it he had a proof text for the calling he had received to run the Gentile mission. Under no circumstances did Gentiles need to join with Israel by conversion in order to be part of the consummation, the salvation, and the age to come.

A typical example of how one can read "deep things" into texts comes at the end of Romans 3. There Paul says "Do we then do away with the law? No, we uphold the law." If one translates the idea correctly it should read, "Do we then make the law obsolete? No. See Genesis 15." What we have here is a *reference* to another passage, not a deep passage about upholding the law by doing away with the law, a paradoxical notion that seems to thrill theologians. Such paradoxes are wonderful, but sometimes they are of our own making.

The central passage for all discussions about Paul and Israel comes at the end of the epistle to the Romans. Paul never uses the term "Israel" in any other sense than to mean the Jewish people seen from within and by itself. It is interesting in the Hellenistic material from this period and in apocryphal writings like First Maccabees, for example, that when Jews speak, the word they use is always "Israel," and when outsiders speak about Israel the phrase is always "the Jews." That is also, by and large, the language used in the synoptic Gospels.

At this point Paul will discuss Israel, not Jews and Greeks, not circumcision and non-circumcision. By his very choice of language he signals that he is now dealing with the question of what his mission means for the ultimate outcome of God's promises, which are to him *by definition* God's promises to Israel. Many people translate Galatians 6:16 as if Paul used the word "Israel" as a term for the Church. But those who read it that way have one too many "ands" in their translation. The text actually says, "Those who live according to my standards, peace be upon them, and mercy upon the house of Israel." If you say, "peace and mercy be upon them, *and* upon the house of Israel," that is one "and" too many. The passage means, "I pray peace upon them, and I pray mercy upon the house of Israel." Israel is always Israel for Paul.

Paul's Epistle to the Romans has become, theologically, his most important legacy. It was actually *meant* to be a kind of penultimate legacy, because Paul wrote to the church in Rome when he thought he had finished his apostolic work in the eastern part of the Mediterranean. Still, he had his mind set on going to Spain. He wrote to Rome in order to inform the church there about his missionary theology, his apostolic strategy. He wanted the community to know all about it, since now he would be going to the western part of the empire, on the other side of Rome. In the fifteenth chapter, he stressed with words upon words that he had no interest in telling the Romans anything—how to live, or how to think, or what to do. He was saying, "I only deal with those congregations I have started myself, and I will just come through, just stop in transit. I have no intention of doing anything else but visiting with you and mutually lifting up one another. Do not think that I am coming to interfere in the affairs of the church in Rome."

So then why did Paul write? He wanted Rome to know his thinking about his mission, and how that mission fits into what God is doing in the world. He started to explain it, and then finally he came to the question, "But what about Israel?" Israel does not seem to think that Jesus is the Messiah. This bothered Paul exceedingly, not because his ego was hurt. That would have played into his almost insatiable arrogance. His own mission was going very well, but Peter's mission to the Jews was not, according to Paul's way of thinking. No, there was a *deeper* question for Paul here: Can you trust God? God's promise to Israel seemed firm and clear; it could not be abridged. So Paul began to make all kinds of arguments. He was upset; we can even see that in the syntax of his sentences. He seeks other examples where God's freedom strikes us as odd—the choice of Jacob instead of Esau, the use of Pharaoh, the metaphors of the potter and the pots—and he goes on and on and on. Ultimately it all leads to the view that, contrary to what he and others had expected, somehow God had made a change.

It might not be attractive to the philosophers among us to have the Bible say that God's mind can change, and I don't think Maimonides delighted in the thought, but Paul says it seems that God has put Israel on hold.

The interesting thing about Romans 9–11, as it looked to Christians then, is that the stiff-necked refusal of the Jews to accept Jesus as the Messiah led to invectives; the anger and the disappointment already present within the Gospel traditions took the form of strong condemnation and vilification. Not so with Paul, the apostle to the Gentiles: "Did the Jews then stumble on the stone [Isaiah 28] in order to fall? Oh no, no! It was to your glory." The Jews in God's plan somehow strangely had to step aside for a little while so that the Gentiles had time to come in. That is Paul's model, his construct, and he expresses it in many ways. The "no" of the Jews made the "yes" of the Gentiles possible. Paul struggled with the texts, and that is what he came up with. But he doesn't end there. The most moving part of Paul's dealing with Israel is precisely that he is not through yet. The end of his reflections on Israel consists of his tearing into the Gentile church and Gentile Christians, accusing them of contempt toward the people of Israel.

Paul perceived the first signs of Christian anti-Semitism. He was the first theologian who saw the specter of gruesome things to come. Again he piled up images, and they are not always successful. There is grafting, and there are roots, and there are branches, and there are the first fruits, and there is the dough offered first. Paul just poured out all these images, but there is no question what they mean.

Sometimes when we read Paul we have to read the beginning of a passage and the end of the passage, and then trust that he *thinks* he has come from the beginning to the end by way of what he says in between, though that isn't always so clear. Paul, like us, must have had good days and bad days, and we should remember that these texts were dictated, not "penned," as precious students like to write in their papers.

All of Paul's manifold images are aimed at telling the Gentiles to stand in awe, to understand that they are borne by the root, and not the other way around. These images teach respect for Israel. In the decisive verse

Paul says, "I will tell you a secret lest you be conceited." And the secret is that all Israel will be saved. Why does Paul say that? By "all Israel" he means not only those out of Israel, like himself, who had accepted Jesus as the Messiah. It was inconceivable for Paul that there could be an end to God's mending of the creation without the saving of all Israel. Clearly he says, "Out of Zion comes the one who delivers." This is an intentional misquotation; the Septuagint says "for the sake of Zion," and the Hebrew text says "to Zion." But the fact that salvation has to do with Zion is important to Paul. It is exactly as John 4 says: "For salvation comes from the Jews."

Paul carried the argument further, suggesting that the Gentiles were not fit to lecture the Jews, perhaps not even fit to run a mission to the Jews. Finally he wrote a doxology, the only doxology Paul ever wrote in God-language, without any mention of Christ or Jesus: "Oh the depth of the riches and the wisdom and the knowledge of God, how unsearchable are his judgments and how inscrutable his ways." Thus Paul's presentation ends with a reference to a mystery that makes the haughty and conceited thoughts of Christians toward the Jewish people just as ugly as they are. Paul foresaw the apparition of supersession and contempt for the Jews, and he called it a mystery. When I teach this, many Christian theologians say, "You teach two ways of salvation, one for Jews and one for Christians." But I do no such thing. I would just call this arrangement God's "traffic plan." And Paul called it a mystery.

I have noted Paul's difficulty accepting his weakness. After all that has transpired in the history of Jews and Christians, perhaps this Christian conceit toward Israel was a sort of mental imperialism that had to be replaced by weakness, according to God's will. One can ask why Paul—this super missionary who was tested sorely for his convictions and certainly proved that he was not ashamed of the Gospel—was the only one who really warned Christians expressly against false missionary zeal. I think there is a psychological answer to this question. Paul had already been burned once. He had persecuted the Christian community out of religious zeal, and he was not going to let history repeat itself.

We can use Paul's idea of mystery as a model for thinking about the mystery of the outcome of our witness—by life, obedience, and words, Jewish and Christian both. How God will use that witness is a mystery, and it does not befit us to describe it in terms of our own victories. We shall have to learn a weakness of another kind, just as Paul learned about a different sort of weakness.

2
A Particular Letter and Sin Universal: Romans 1:1—3:20 and 15

There are few epistles to which we bring as much baggage as Paul's Epistle to the Romans. Due to its glory and power, its importance in Christian history, its dearness to the heart, and its fascinating puzzlement to the mind, it has attracted interpretations upon interpretations upon interpretations through the ages. My first admonition to those who read it is to forget everything they know about it.

The recipients of this epistle presumably had not read any Gospel, or any of Paul's other epistles. They certainly had not read the Gospels in the form we have them, and Romans came to them as a letter.

One can argue whether it is just a matter of high style to call Paul's writings epistles rather than letters. "Letter" is perhaps the best word to use for real letters of the sort we write our friends. "Epistle" is the best word for a communication in the form of a letter that is either a think piece or a literary genre.

Paul's letter to Philemon is, to be sure, a letter, and Paul did not have the slightest inkling that it would make the Bible. He did not know that any of his letters would do so, as we well know. Hebrews and James are perhaps the most epistolary writings of the New Testament, and Romans is the most epistolary of the writings that are certainly by Paul himself. I have some doubts about Colossians and Ephesians, but I have no doubt that Corinthians, Galatians, Romans and Philippians are written by Paul, even if Philippians is a composite.

When we ask what Romans is about, we have to forget all the other epistles, because to harmonize or homogenize them is the surest road to confusion. The letters are different in terminology, for example. The typical Pauline model of justification by faith occurs only in Romans and Galatians. It plays no part whatsoever in 1 Cor-inthians, and has a somewhat different connotation in 2 Corinthians. There is also a glimpse of it in Philippians.

Paul's thought is *ad hoc.* He is writing, and unlike some of us preachers, he knows what he wants. He is not just mouthing beautiful thoughts. He has a purpose. Here we are going after the purpose of Paul's Epistle to the Romans.

Lutheran tradition just knows that the purpose of Romans is to teach justification by faith without the works of the law. Calvinists just know that it is the chief text from which to get the proper doctrine of predestination, and Catholic tradition takes the second chapter as its chief text for substantiating its glorious and correct doctrine of natural law. Augustine, by mistranslating, found the doctrine of original sin in chapter five.

It is reasonable to anticipate that Romans has a limited scope. We can actually gauge the purpose of Romans better than any of Paul's other epistles. We know fairly well the purpose of 1 Corinthians, but we know it by inference. We know what Paul says, and from it we infer the situation to which he spoke.

In Romans Paul's purpose in writing is crystal clear. From Romans 15:17 on we are told directly what the situation is. Paul says that he is through with his mission to the East. It has not been saturation evangelism exactly, but he has placed enough beacons, significant communities, and gatherings of the elect, in some of the major Eastern centers, all the way, he says, from Jerusalem to Illyricum (Yugoslavia). Now he has finished in the East, and is going West.

One of the reasons Paul gives for being through with the East is worth noting. "It has always been my principle to work where nobody else has worked," he says. This is an expression of the pioneering spirit—"Don't dig in old places, but move on." It suggests that there were many places that had been missionized by others. That is important, because we always have the feeling, especially in the Protestant tradition, that Paul was the one who brought Christianity to the Gentiles. We know from the Book of Acts, however, that Peter was the first missionary who baptized the Gentiles.

In any case, Paul is moving West. He has plans to go to Spain, and on the way he hopes to visit Rome. That is clearly the reason for his writing. I am not discussing footnotes here, nor am I discussing the rather intriguing and very complex argument of T.W. Manson, who has looked at the different endings of Romans, and where the doxologies fall in those last chapters.[1] He has put all the evidence together to suggest that what we have in Romans 1–15 is a think-piece epistle as it reached Rome, but it was actually meant as a more general epistle. We have the Roman copy, so to speak. Therefore, he argues, one should not interpret Romans from the point of view of a letter written to the Church in Rome, because it functions also as a general epistle.

There is something attractive in this, and there is even interesting textual evidence for it in Codex G, where the references to Rome are missing. I think, however, this is best explained by the desire to make Romans a general epistle. We know from the Muratorian Fragment that the early Christians already pondered the theological question, "How can a letter written to a specific church be a letter to the church at large?" So we have no reference to Ephesus in the letter to the Ephesians in most of the manuscripts, and we can explain that. They were smart, those early Christians. They solved the problem by saying that Paul addressed seven churches. The Book of Revelation addressed seven churches, and the Book of Revelation is *the* revelation. Hence it is acceptable. Perhaps the early Christians answered the question in an unusual way, but at least they thought about it.

In any case, Paul is writing with a clear anticipation of going West, his eastern ministry having come to an end. There is a constant emphasis in chapter 15 on the fact that he is only coming to visit. "I have no authority in Rome at all," he says. Paul reiterates that he will only meet them in transit. "We will refresh one another a little, but I have no authority over you," he writes. Already in Chapter 1 he says, "I have always wished to come so that I could impart some gifts," and then he stops himself and says, "That's not the way to say it. I say, rather, we can exchange our gifts mutually" (1:12). He is very conscious of not pressing himself on the Church in Rome. "It has always been my principle not to dabble in situations where churches have been founded by others," he says. We have the same situation from the other side in 1 Corinthians where Paul says, "You have many *pedagogoi*, but you have only one father, because I begat you."

This issue is important to Paul. He does not have the "father" relation to the church in Rome. In 15:15 he reminds them, "I have spoken very boldly. You are doing okay. I know for sure that you are wonderful, and I am just reminding you." Paul has no authority. He is in transit. He is going to be speeded on by the Romans, and he is going to enjoy their company only for a little while.

First, however, Paul has to go to Jerusalem, presumably to deliver the collection he has mentioned already in Galatians, the only thing he had promised to do at the Apostolic Council. The Book of Acts tells us something different. Paul had promised only to remember the poor, a reference to the Church in Jerusalem. For him this collection had enormous symbolic significance. He is afraid he will get into trouble in Jerusalem, and he is unsure the Jerusalem leadership will welcome his coming or the gifts with which he comes. But he hopes they will, so that when he visits Rome, he will come in full and happy joy. Paul invites the Romans to battle with him in his ministry through prayer. He describes his relation to Rome with great care, not lording it over them, not instructing them, not lecturing them, but preaching to them, being charismatic with them.

Thus, Paul is writing this epistle at a crucial juncture in his mission. In it he reflects upon his mission within the total plan of God. He is not teaching, he is not instructing. The letter is an account of his mission—*apologia pro vita et via sua*, a kind of apology for or explanation of how he sees his own mission, which God has given him to carry out as the apostle to the Gentiles. This motif is totally clear in Galatians 1, where Paul says that he did not receive his call through any kind of tradition, but, rather, he has it straight from God. He uses the analogy of the call of Jeremiah, who was already formed as a prophet in his mother's womb, and he quotes Jeremiah to present his direct line. His call to be the apostle to the Gentiles is what the letter to the Romans is about. In chapter 15 his apostolic mission is seen as a priestly service, rendering the Gentiles to God. The symbol of that service is rendering the collection of the Gentile churches, which he is bringing now to Jerusalem. That is very clear. Paul is the apostle to the Gentiles.

This letter is from A to Z a letter about mission. It is a theology of the Pauline mission to the Gentiles, and its climax comes in chapters 9–11, where Paul reflects upon how this mission to the Gentiles relates to the people of Israel. That is Paul's agenda. The letter is written either with Rome in mind, or to the Gentile Christians in Rome directly.

Romans and Galatians have many similar arguments. They both discuss law and justification, and use the same passage from Habakkuk: "for the righteous will live by faith." The big difference between them is that in Galatians Paul is speaking to one of his own congregations, in which a certain kind of Jewish Christianity had made inroads that pressed the Gentiles to accept Jewish ways and a Jewish lifestyle. Galatians was written against Judaizing Gentile Christians. It is a ferocious letter and the only one in which Paul gives no thanks in his prayers for those to whom he writes. All his other letters contain the wonderful formulaic words, "I always give thanks to God in my prayers for you." Exactly at that point in Galatians Paul says "I am surprised that you have fallen so low."

In Romans we are not dealing with Judaizing Christians. The word *Judaioi* occurs in Romans, it means Jews—*bona fide* Jewish Jews—and the discussion in Romans has to do with Jews and Gentiles, not with Judaizing Christians over against non-Judaizing Christians. That is why Galatians and Romans, though similar, are so drastically different.

The Romans Debate, edited by Karl Donfried, contains an article that makes the very precise historical suggestion that Paul writes his epistle to the Romans at the very time in Roman history when the emperor Claudius promulgated an edict that kicked the Jews, or at least the Jewish leadership, out of Rome in the year 49.[2] But already in the 50s, during the early years of Nero, the Jewish community had started to come back into Rome, and was even invited back by Nero. That would then be exactly the situation when Paul wrote to Rome, and it would mean that for a while the Church in Rome was a Gentile church, which did not have any Jews around. To use the terrible Nazi word, Rome had been *Judenrein*, free of Jews. Because they started to come back, Paul had to raise this question, which weighed so heavily on his mind—what now about the relation between the Gentile Christians and the Jewish community?

The epistle to the Romans deals with real Jews and real Gentile Christians. That can be seen in the very way Paul states "I am aware of the fact that I speak to people who are not under the law." Those people are the Gentiles. He introduces his epistle in chapter 1 by saying, "We who have received grace and apostolic ministry to the obedience of faith among all the Gentiles for his name's sake, among whom are also you who are in Rome." He only addresses himself to those who are Gentiles because he has no say over the others.

Without being pedantic, in Romans Paul is seeking clarification, understanding, and support. Pedantry is the chief sin of exegetes. It is amazing how our spiritual faith and theological greed make us pedantic in our dealing with the Scriptures. That is not so strange. That is our way of paying homage to the Scriptures. We press down on it, since we think it is ten times deeper than it is. If it is the word of God it has to be at least as deep as I can be, and then some. This may well be our chief reason for not having the capacity to read the text. Let us use a light touch in our serious reading of the epistle to the Romans.

In Romans the principle of justification by faith is a principle of mission—of understanding how it is possible for Gentiles to become part of God's scheme, and plan, and people. How can the Gentiles be children of God, children of Abraham? Paul uses the phrase "Abba, Father" twice, in Galatians and in Romans. What he gets out of the "abba" is not the warm, romantic interpretation you have in Joachim Jeremias' book.[3] The only thing Paul means by "abba" is, "if we say 'abba' we are fallen heirs to the promises of old, and to God's will." "Abba" is a question of heirs—who are to be heirs or children of Abraham? The crucial argument is found in Paul's exegesis of Abraham. He believed, and it was a saving grace. He believed, and it was "counted unto righteousness."

This is Paul's wonderful discovery, that Abraham believed before he was circumcised. The circumcision did not come before that passage but it came after. Thus we are justified by faith on the model of Abraham, without circumcision. That is how the argument about justification by faith functions. It is hammered out on the anvil of the question: how can Gentiles become part of God's people? Some Christians think that the doctrine of justification by faith is the answer to the question of the plagued conscience: how can I be sure of God's grace? Answer: through faith. But that was not Paul's idea. Paul never had any problem with his conscience in that sense. He knew that he had been perfect according to the law. He was a terrible bragger. He was always the greatest of sinners, the greatest of apostles. He speaks in tongues more than anybody else. His struggle, his weakness, and his epileptic condition, or whatever it was, make for an interesting personal drama from which we learn much. His *theologia crucis* is grounded in it. But his justification by faith argument has nothing to do with it. It is related to the question of his mission argument for the status of his Gentile converts before God and as members of the people of God. That is precisely what justification by faith is all about—his ministry and his mission.

The first sections of all Paul's epistles have much in common. They have a certain form, a certain shape, partly built on the epistolary form of the times and partly on Paul's "twang" and Paul's way, since he was a very arrogant, egocentric person. He did not just want to write in the conventional manner; he wanted to make his writing his own, to give it a kind of Pauline zing, and he did. Since all his epistles are more or less written on the same pattern, their differences are revealing. Paul Schubert has argued that these little ingressions show that from the beginning Paul knows what he is up to.[4] He gives away his main point. In the letter to Galatia, for example, he has the usual introduction— that he is called apostle, and so on—but he says, "apostle of Jesus Christ not through people but through Christ himself." This is then the theme of his critique of those who see him as subservient to the Jerusalem church. It is spelled out right there in the very formulaic language. Hence it is rather striking that already in 1 Corinthians Paul says what he usually says in his ingressions, but he adds that note—right in the first words, about the togetherness of all the churches, the kind that comes in the body.

Two things stand out in Romans. One is that Paul is using a precreedal theological formula that is not his usual habit. He is going Catholic, so to speak. He is writing outside of his domain, and he is anxious to place himself and the church under the creed that holds the church together. He is doing this also for another reason. It is a way of bringing in the dimension of Israel, and hence he uses the faith formula that is presumably not of his own making but must be early, because it is straight adoptionism from the christological point of view—as the early church always was. Adoptionism means to think of Christ as having been made Lord and Messiah in his resurrection, or somewhere along the line—not being eternal from the beginning, but rather adopted into the Godhead, into divinity.

According to this formula—Jesus Christ who was the son of David according to the flesh and "proven" or "set aside" (there are all kinds of translations here), the son of God in power according to the spirit of holiness by the resurrection from the dead—it is out of his resurrection with the spirit that he is the son of God. That is an early formula, but it is not really Pauline language. Paul has received apostleship, and the specific task of his apostleship is to bring about the obedience of faith among all the Gentiles for Christ's name. Among these are "all of you who are in Rome, the called and beloved ones of Jesus Christ." So here Paul thinks of Rome as the Gentile church.

He goes on to say that he has not forgotten them. A note here even suggests that Paul is thinking, "How can I get to Jerusalem with a collection from the Gentiles, the symbolic gift, and not have Rome, the super Gentile power city, represented? Have I slighted them?" In verse 13 Paul says he had wanted so much to come. He always speaks about this, and we know from other writings both of Paul and in Acts that his illness caused him to change his travel plans. He says in Galatians, "You were wonderful, you Galatians, in those good old days when you accepted my word as the word of God, although I was stranded in Galatia for sickness's sake." And in Thessalonians, he tells about how he had planned to come but Satan hindered him. The Book of Acts, which is so pious, translates that idea into "the Holy Spirit did not allow us to come." But Paul says: "Satan hindered us." Just as an angel of Satan smote Paul in the face, his thorn in the flesh is his bad health.

Paul might have been thinking, "How can I go and deliver the gift of the Gentiles, having not even been in touch with Rome? In verse 13 he says "I had wanted to come, that I have some fruit (*karpos*) from you as from the other Gentiles." In 1 Corinthians 15 he also uses the word *karpos* about the collection, which of course also stands for the sacrifice with the wonderful fragrance that he as the priest, the apostle of the Gentiles, offers to God. "I do not want to give you anything. I just want to have a mutual sharing," Paul says.

But the Romans should not think that Paul is scared. He is quite bold and willing to bring the Gospel, and he says a most surprising thing that exegetes have never quite solved: "I have obligations both to Greeks and to barbarians." That is an odd way of addressing the Romans if you want to be listened to. Or had the condescension that is typical of Hellenistic cultural imperialism gone out of the word "barbarians?" There is a discussion in Cicero about how people used this word for everybody, and also for those in Rome.[5] Paul says, "I am not afraid of the Gospel. It is the power of God toward salvation, for everyone who believes, be it the Jew first, and also the Greek. For the righteousness, the justice, the rightness, the *dikaiosyne* of God, is revealed through faith for faith."

To say that in the church we have "righteousness," and in the world we have "justice" is to play a popular language game. Of course in Latin both are covered by *justitia.* When Luther came to his breakthrough about justification by faith, he did not have the language distinction between righteousness and justice. Righteousness is justice in all respects. Justice is righteousness; *dikaiosyne* is when God has put things right. The first occurrence of this word *dikaiosyne* (*sedaqah* in Hebrew) is in the oldest fragment of poetry we have in the Bible—at least according to many Old Testament scholars—in the song of Deborah, the ferocious woman minister who was actually the first of the prophets. In her song "they rehearse the righteous acts of God," as the King James version puts it (Judges 5:11). The Revised Standard Version uses "triumphs." *Sedaqah* means victory. It means God has finally put the whole world right. "The righting of things" catches much of the sense. Putting things right, *all* things, not just the soul game, and not just the political situation, but all things—that is the meaning of *dikaiosyne.* For the righting of God is revealed in the Gospel, "from faith to faith," as it is written, *ho de dikaios ek pisteos zesetai.* We usually say "and the righteous shall live by faith." I would translate it, "the righteous will live by faith." In the third person you express straight future by "will," and Paul reads this as a statement about the future. "For that time will come"—not as a principle, but as a statement—"the time toward which the whole world is moving, when there will be this living by faith." Now, if we understand it that way we see a direct link with Romans 3:21—"But now without the law *a* righteousness (we should translate "*a* righteousness," I think, and not use the translation "*the* [Protestant] righteousness") of God has been revealed, and witnessed..." God's righting of the whole cosmos is actually what this statement looks toward.

Paul demonstrates in chapters 1 and 2 that the world is in a mess, and that human beings are responsible for this mess. Time and time again he makes the point that human beings are without excuse. They should have known better. Had they just used the kind of knowledge given to them by God, they could have done better. But they started to worship the created world instead of the Creator, and they practiced homosexuality. This is the stereotype of Hellenistic Judaism in Greek culture. Paul says that not only do they have human pictures of God, but they also have images of reptiles and birds. Perhaps he is thinking a little about influences from Egypt.

In any case he uses the standard slander of the other, the typical perception, "we don't, they do." They practice idolatry, and exchange the natural for the unnatural, which is the typical argument against homosexuality. Paul uses this standard argument. Then he rounds it off in 1:32 by saying that they should have known better. Not only do they do these terrible things, but they live in a culture that condones them. Not only do they do it themselves, but they also condone those who practice such acts. This is a negative picture of the world in which we live. It isn't "righted"—it is not the right way.

Paul continues in chapter 2 to say that even those who judge are not doing so well. This is one of the few passages in Paul that is strongly reminiscent of some gospel material, especially from John the Baptist. In 2:4 he asks, "Don't they understand that God's patience is meant to drive toward *metanoia*?" Paul is moving in his thought toward the question: "Where then are the Jews? They don't have idols as a people; they do not condone homosexuality and presumably practice it very little." Then Paul uses a common Jewish trick. He blames the home folk with the good example of others. Paul says, "Those Gentiles aren't so bad." He turns the whole argument around and says, "They are a law unto themselves. They are not without a conscience. They actually fulfill many aspects of the law."

The main argument is clear. In some way the Gentiles have it over Israel. There are not only the righteous Gentiles whom Jewish teaching speaks about, but there is also this question, which you have in the Pharisees and in the teachings of Jesus: "Do not the Gentiles do the same? Why do you think you are so great?" This is a good Jewish teaching technique—to turn the tables.

In Romans 2:17 Paul addresses himself specifically to the Jewish situation, to those who claim that they have the law, even the very shape and form of the will of God, of knowledge, and of truth. Then Paul says, "You who teach the others, why don't you teach yourself?" I read this as a question. "You who preach not to steal, do you steal?" I always loved that line for *kerygma* preachers. The word for "preach" here is *kerysso*, and despite all the *kerygma* theories of what preaching really is, I have never heard anyone use this example to say that "do not steal" is the *kerygma*, but that is what Paul says.

"You who say 'do not commit adultery,' commit adultery. You who speak negatively about idols, you actually practice idolatry." What Paul means here is that Israel is not perfect. There is nothing psychological in this at all. It is not that in a deeper sense you break the law. That is not part of Paul's argument. That does not make sense in the context. His point is, we haven't yet reached the *dikaiosyne*, that righting and rightness. After that he makes the statement that the true Jew is not the external Jew. He does not deny the theoretical possibility of the circumcised person who fulfills the law, but he looks at Israel as a whole, as he has looked at the Gentiles as a whole. This is curious, because exegetes have usually recognized that Paul speaks about the Gentiles in great generalities. But he also thinks about the Jews as a whole, and he says the kingdom has not come yet. That is not news. That is not being nasty to the Jews; that was also what the Pharisees taught. There is sin in the community, of course. So apparently the *soteria* (salvation) of which Habakkuk spoke has not arrived yet.

In Romans 3 Paul asks, "What is the advantage of being a Jew?" It is plentiful, he says, and he goes on to make a very simple point. On the way, however, he gets a little bogged down. The best way to read him is to see what question he asks at the beginning of the paragraph, and then where he comes out at the end. He usually sets up his arguments that way. He asks a question, and he summarizes an answer. You might not like the way that he handles it, but he thinks that he gets from that first point to the last point by what lies in between. One must try to unearth his line of thought.

Paul is going to prove that the whole world is in terrible shape, and he is going to clinch the argument with a couple of gruesome quotations of how wicked the world is. Then he sums up by saying, "For we know that there is no perfection on earth at all." Thus, it seems to Paul that no flesh is put totally right by the works of the law. Rather, what comes from the law, he says, seems to be the knowledge and awareness of sin, of our imperfection. We are in a mess, and we are responsible for it. Both Jews and Gentiles. Whenever Paul is about to clinch his argument in Romans, he almost always repeats that phrase, "both Jews and Gentiles," or "first the Jews, then the Gentiles." This is to remind Lutherans what his argument is all about, rather than all those sermons about sin and guilt and forgiveness that Lutherans cherish.

Paul anticipates that the Romans have an image of him (3:7). They have heard about this awesome Paul. After all, he was a sophisticated fellow, an operator among operators. Paul says: "God has strange ways of acting. If one really follows the principle I have stated before [and it comes back in chapter 6], one could think I teach that if now God's truth becomes apparent through my lying, I'd better lie all the more so that the truth shines better. If God works in that funny way," Paul writes, "should we then sin the more that grace might abound?"

Paul teaches that we must learn to distinguish between macro-theology and micro-theology, that we will see this in relation to the Jews. "Did the Jews stumble in order to fall? Did Israel stumble in order to fall? No, no, no. They stumbled in order that the gospel would come to you." The more we sin, and the more sin there is, the more God uses it toward glorification.

Paul has this peculiar way of thinking, and he says that it led some people to blaspheme and to claim that he teaches that we should do evil in order that good may come. But Paul says that is crazy. Their judgment is certainly just, he says. "Do we Jews then have an advantage? Not really, because I have already laid the charge on both Jews and Greeks, that they and we are all under sin." This enormously important thought—that God doesn't act in a straight line, and that the more sin increases, the more grace increases—has already surfaced. But woe onto you, says Paul, if you assign that pattern of thinking to individual living. Such thinking is a macro model, but it cannot be applied on the micro level.

This is what Paul will be saying in chapter 6 with great clarity. That's why he says, "It might seem that way to you if you think that you can take my macro theology and translate it into pastoral counseling. But that is wrong. This is big stuff. I am writing to you about the mysterious ways in which God works in the cosmos and in history." That is what Romans is about.

3

Paul's Exegetical Find, Its Consequences and Limits—The By-passing of Moses and the Macro/Micro Distinction: Romans 3:21—8:39

I have suggested that in the Epistle to the Romans Paul is putting forward the best possible case for his mission and his ministry. This is not to say that certain issues in the epistle may not have more general theological ramifications. But do not worry too much about relevance. It doesn't seem to us to be a major problem that the Gentiles should be in on God's plan. To us that seems relatively unnecessary to argue for fifteen chapters. A greedy hunger for relevance often blinds the eyes of preachers and theologians.

These days the new resources of ore and mineral riches on the great continent of Australia are spotted not by teams with Geiger counters but by satellites. One has to get quite a distance away in order to see them. There is a way in which we also need some distance when we read the Bible, and anyone who worries about relevance is not a Christian, at least not a biblical Christian. If we tag on our own little relevancies, we undercut the authority of the Word. We have to stay with it until it opens up what it is, not what it becomes by our cleverness.

People go away from a sermon in one of two ways. Either we say: Wasn't he or she clever? Who could get all that out of that passage? Or we go home and look at the Scripture and say: Now I see what has been there all the time. There is added artifice. That is the sort of distance we need.

In the first large section of Paul's letter to the Romans (1:18—3:20), for his own and for obvious reasons Paul has given a mighty panorama of the disorder in which the world finds itself. It is a confused and muddled world in which the minor differences between those who have the Torah in its fullness, the Jewish people, and the Gentiles, become surprisingly insignificant. His point is that in the larger scheme the variations become minor, although he says "now do the Jews have an advantage—oh, plenty." As Paul looks at it, it seems a minor variation compared with the possibility which in Romans 3:20 is around the corner. Paul believes in an eschatological fact and event—namely that the righteousness of God has been revealed. Actually, says Paul, what came through the law seems to be *epignosis hamartias*—awareness of sin.

In my exegetical habits I am a minimalist. I also think that we reach the best translation by toning down the text rather than by toning it up. Most exegetes are maximalists, especially when they deal with texts they like. That is to say, when they come upon the word *epignosis*, many people turn to Gerhard Kittel or to their own homemade etymologies, as if *epignosis* means something considerably deeper than *gnosis* because it is a little longer. But *epignosis* means awareness, a cooler word than *gnosis*. That awareness will be Paul's theme in Romans 7, and he has already flagged it in this statement in 3:20: what seems to come from the law is *epignosis*, the awareness of sin.

Then follows the statement that the righteousness of God has been revealed. For Paul, this is not a new understanding, but actually the righteousness of God which has become manifest as had been promised both in the Torah (in the Pentateuch, as we say), and in the prophets. For Paul that just means Scripture. Righteousness of God comes through faith in Jesus, or through that faith which Jesus has, or through that faith that somehow is Jesus. In Galatians Paul speaks about *pistis* (faith) as if he could just as well say Christ. "Until faith came," he says, instead of saying, "until Christ came." Christian faith is not an attitude for Paul. It is not some holy rope trick. It is the opportunity that is given to humanity when there exists the possibility of embracing Jesus as the Messiah. Faith is defined by its object.

Paul says again that this faith is available to all who believe, without distinction, for all have sinned and are lacking the glory of God. I am inclined to follow those exegetes who say that this statement is a reference to the *imago*, the *doxa*. Such a statement when spoken in relation to people like the Romans seems in this Jewish Hellenistic Greek age to refer to the loss of the image of God, about which Paul spoke so impressively in the beginning of the negative section about righteousness in Romans. This lack, this loss or absence, this minus, is restored *gratis* in Jesus Christ. Here, as in the beginning of the first chapter, Paul draws on traditional formulations.

As to where, exactly, the fragment of the traditional creedal statement begins and ends within 3:21–26, go to the commentaries and read the discussion. But Paul is clearly using language that he uses nowhere else, and that is shaped in Christian tradition prior to Paul. Perhaps it is a formula that he anticipates will be known in Rome, and he wants to speak in language familiar to the Romans. For example, very seldom does Paul speak about the blood of Christ. Yet here he plays on the image of the mercy seat which the high priest approached on the most holy day, sprinkling blood and performing the act of atonement. What is perhaps even more important than the rareness of blood language in Paul is that if I, a Lutheran, were Paul, this is, of course, where I would say something about the cross. But there is not one reference to the cross in Romans. The cross actually belongs primarily to the Corinthian cycle of Paul's writing. Wouldn't this be a perfect passage in a proper Pauline way for reflections on the cross? But instead we get the mercy seat (*hilasterion*). Paul plays on language which he has received from the tradition. Then he says that this is a marvelous time; God has kept his cool until this time. The *paresis* is God's passing over sins. God could have come, of course, and intervened at any time, but God has held back until this very time, until there was, in God's plan, this moment—the moment of the new eschatological dispensation.

For Paul the importance of the new dispensation is the sense that since it is linked to Christ, there is no *diastole* (distinction), no *prosopolempsia* (partiality). All are treated alike. He presents the christological language of atonement for a very specific purpose: just as we are sinners, a condition that unites us all in this confusion, so there is the one without distinction who gives salvation now (*en to nyn kairo*).

From a hermeneutical point of view, it is always very interesting when the New Testament says "now" (Rom. 3:21). If the text says "now" in year 56 of the Common Era, where does that leave you and me? It leaves us almost 2000 years later. No kerygmatic gamesmanship can overcome that simple fact. What is "now" in the Scriptures is "then" in the now. There are no tricks, not even a reference to the fact that the Jewish people in their seders help themselves as in that very night getting out of Egypt. Of course they do. Celebration is about that kind of identification, but it is not anything more. Paul was speaking about this mighty "now" which for him was a "now" that can never be repeated. It was once for all, and we relate to it living on its fruits rather than trying to create some "Bibleland" or trying to play at some Pauline identification. Paul spoke about specific periods of time, and they remain specific periods.

Paul's language in 3:26 is also not very typical language for him, but it has become very dear language to later theological traditions. C. E. B. Cranfield in his two-volume *International Critical Commentary* on Romans has a wonderful way of giving all the alternatives for passages, and then knocking them off one after the other with his very good knowledge of Greek and Greek literature. Combine his work with the commentary of Ernst Käsemann, who was a man with purpose and hence none of the patience of an Oxford don.

Those two commentaries supplement each other very well. Käsemann had a sensitivity to pre-Pauline tradition and what Paul did with it, which is underdeveloped, to say the least, in Cranfield. Cranfield read Romans on one level, without overtones and understatements. There is also a major article by Sammy K. Williams in the *Journal of Biblical Literature* (1980) on Abraham as the key not only to Romans but also to Paul's understanding of the justification by faith.[6]

Williams writes that *pistis Christou* means faith *of* Christ and not faith *in* Christ, and that "faith in Christ" is the *lectio difficilior* from all points of view. It is very difficult to use objective genitives in that kind of combination when referring to a person. If Williams is right, and if there are elements here in which we really have a clear idea of that faith *of* Jesus—Jesus' stance, so to say—then the idea of both being the just one and justifying others becomes much more natural. It is worth noting that in Romans 8, the passage "he overcame this tragedy by sending his son in the flesh" also makes "faith *of* Jesus" a very natural way of reading. Paul does speak here in both ways.

Paul's point in Romans 3 is not to teach a specific doctrine of atonement, reconciliation or redemption. He uses a rich, conflated image, and his point is one to which he returns in verse 27. "Where then is the bragging (*kaukesis*)"—bragging in the sense of feeling superior to the other. That's what bragging is about, isn't it? Bragging is cut out, Paul says. By what law? By the law of works? By the law of circumcision or food laws, the laws that set people apart? No, by the law of faith.

At this point comes an introduction. The whole section, Romans 3:21–31, should perhaps best be seen as a preface to chapter 4, because Paul is going to bring in his biblical argument for God now, having offered a way of access that makes Jews and Gentiles equal. The passage is a powerful preface to using the example of Abraham. How do I know that? Partly because in verse 28 we meet for the first time the word *logizometha gar*: for we reckon, we interpret, we read so as to recognize, we discern, we count things this way—that a human being (*anthropos*) is justified by faith without the works of the law. For God isn't only the God of the Jews, is he? No, he is also the God of the Gentiles.

Here we have a good Jewish teaching, grounded in the simple fact that God is one. We are dealing in a period when oneness was the same as holiness. This age, more or less on its way toward Plotinus, was hypnotized by oneness. Paul used the "oneness" argument himself, in Galatians 3, when he said that Moses was an intermediary, and an intermediary implies more than one; but God is one. That infatuation with oneness created all kinds of interesting theological reflection. Paul uses it in Romans in a light vein: of course God is one, so God is the one who justifies on the principle of faith, who puts right the circumcised people, not just in relationship to himself, but in all respects, and also the uncircumcised ones, "the blunt ones" as they were called in the Greek, through that same faith. So Paul also recognizes a distinction.

Do we then do away with the law through this faith? Heavens, no—*me genoito*—one of the few optatives that survives into the holiness of the New Testament, and I have no doubt it should actually be translated "no—see Genesis 15." Rather than do away with the law, we establish the law. *Histano* is equal to the Hebrew *qiyyem*, which is used in scriptural interpretation in mishnaic Hebrew. It means to establish the fulfillment of something, to establish its meaning in the "now." That is what Paul says: "No. We are proving the meaning of the law from Scripture, from Torah, from the Pentateuch itself," and then he cites the passage in Romans 4:3.

There is a lesson here for us exegetes. "Do we do away with the law? No, we *establish* the law in a *deeper* sense." We read this as another example of those wonderful, mysterious words of Paul, but there is no notion of that; Paul is saying, "Cf. Genesis 15." He just did not have that way of citing chapter and verse. At this point Paul thinks of the example of Abraham. He has found in Genesis 15 a choice passage for making his point: Abraham believed in God, trusted in God (*episteusen to theo*), and it was reckoned to him as righteousness. How could Paul be so happy to find such a passage? He says a little, "Have you noticed that this statement comes *before* the passage in Genesis 17 about the circumcision of Abraham? Imagine! Abraham was justified by faith *before* he was circumcised."

This was almost too good to be true for Paul, and it became his central matter. Nine times in this section of Romans he hammers away—*elogiste, elogiste,* "it was reckoned, it was reckoned." That proved it for him—this faith that actually establishes the right situation was given to Abraham when he was a Gentile. That is all Paul has to say. He does elaborate on it—he is a preacher, you know. He just cannot have such a great idea and not make sure that it sinks in.

In the second part of chapter 4, Paul goes on thinking about Abraham. He gets another important theme out of the Abraham passage, and that is the resurrection. Paul read about Abraham's having children when he was almost 100, and about Sarah's "seed" having been made alive, as it says in Hebrews 11:11. Paul had a Galen-like understanding of the procreative process, where the male seed was white and the female seed was red, and when the two seeds came together a human being was created. This miracle between Abraham and Sarah becomes a prototype of the resurrection. The faithfulness of Abraham continued from his believing in God prior to his circumcision into his superhuman capacity to believe in life coming out of a dead body. That is a mighty sermon. The point of the exercise, of course, is obvious. As Paul sums it up at the end of verse 23, this wasn't written only for Abraham's sake; it was counted unto him, reckoned unto him, but it was for us—we to whom it was to be so reckoned, we who believe in him who raised Jesus our Lord from the dead, the one who was handed over for our transgressions' sake and was raised for our justification. Paul rounds out this argument about Abraham, and gets two conclusions out of it: *Abraham is the father in faith of the Gentiles, and he is also the one who points toward the resurrection.*

In Paul's theological thinking there are two spanning arches. There is Abraham-Christ, and there is Adam-Christ. In Romans 5 Paul leaps over to the Adam-Christ arch, describing the radical newness that has come in the eschatological event of Jesus Christ. Just as in Galatians 3 the arch from Abraham to Christ is constructed at the expense of Moses, so the Adam-Christ arch in Romans 5 is also built at the expense of Moses. In 5:13–14 Paul says "so people died before Moses, and they died after Moses. What is the difference? Not much." That is simply his argument. There is *epignosis,* there is awareness, but Moses is consciously bypassed, just as in Galatians 3. The law came 432 years after the promise, and something that follows after in such a fashion cannot change the original testament or promise. After all, the law was given through angels and not really from God directly, and it was given with a time limit—until the coming. In Romans 5 Paul does the same thing, and perhaps the utter belittlement of Moses also occurs in 2 Corinthians 3. But there the counterpart to Moses is not Christ but Paul himself. The ministry of Moses is compared not to Christ, but to the ministry of Paul. Now you might say that to be equal to Paul is perhaps not a belittlement in Paul's mind, but it is certainly not a Moses-Christ typology. Passing over Moses as the divider and diviner in Israel's faith is quite deliberate in Paul's thinking.

I have already spoken about Paul's awareness of the difference between macro and micro patterns of thought. We have a famous passage in Romans 5:20ff. that is very similar to Galatians in some ways. "The law came to increase transgression, but the more sin increased, the more grace increased." This mysterious God does more than merely match sin—that is the nature of grace, and the conclusion leads Paul to the rather reasonable question: "Should we not help God to shine a little?" At one level Paul pursues that thought positively. "This treasure I have in earthen vessels, so that the overwhelming power and glory be shown to be God's and not my own." There, on the weakness theme, his observation actually works. But, Paul says, should we then remain in sin that grace might abound? Of course not.

Theology is tricky. It is not enough just to have ideas and prescriptions. The proof is in the eating, and Paul answers the question he has raised: "Of course that is a ridiculous idea." But how is he going to get out of this line of reasoning? Out of the blue, and in a manner quite rare to Paul, he brings in baptism. He introduces it by playing on the Greek connotation of the word *baptizestai*, which means to drown. Baptism is a word for dying, a word for shipwreck. In Hellenistic Greek it meant death. Interestingly, in the synoptic Gospels there are serious questions whether Jesus said "Can you drink the cup that I drink?" Later this statement was coupled with the saying, "and can you be baptized with the baptism with which I am baptized?" The idea of baptism as death presupposed the play on the Greek word *baptizestai*. This idea so dear to Baptists places them beautifully in line with the Greeks—the idea of death in baptism, or baptism as a symbol of death.

Paul's point, very simply, is that we have to have another image, another concept. We are dealing with something different, and need to get another image into the equation at the micro level, at the level of the individual. Be careful, he warns, because there are dangers and pitfalls in substituting the macro for the micro. Paul then gives his interpretation of dying with Christ and the liberation, the new life that is also new servanthood under God, under Christ, and with Christ. He rounds off this passage in the first part of chapter 7 with a very complicated and perhaps not quite successful argument—a rather contrived argument about the widow who has the right to remarry. At this point Paul can't quite disentangle himself, so we should not try to make his argument work because it really doesn't. He stops with some deep Christian truths, breaking off his imagery in chapter 6. But the new section begins at 7:7.

*

Here we come back to Paul's lengthy explanation of what he has hinted at a few times: "What comes from the law is the awareness of sin." He has said that a couple of times, but now he belabors the thought at some length. The easiest way to read Paul is always to see what questions he raises, and ask what he thinks that he has proven in between. "Is the law sin? Oh no, but I would not have known sin had it not been for the law." How is Paul going to prove that to his own satisfaction? The argument starts with the question, "Is the law sin?" and ends with the statement at verse 12: "I have now proved that the law is holy, and the commandments are holy, righteous and just." Paul proves his argument with the dear old story in Genesis 3.

What we have in verses 7–12 is a midrash on the Fall. It is not unique to Paul. We have similar Jewish homiletical midrashim using this theme. Had it not been for the law, Satan could not have tricked Eve, for example. Paul lifts up that story and says: "So sin took as its starting block, its excuse, its foothold, the commandment." Satan said, "Should God have said to you not to eat of the trees in the garden?" Eve tried to correct that, but Satan was a mighty exegete. Satan tricked humanity by using the law, and had the law not said, "Do not covet, do not desire," Satan could never have got his act going. But that doesn't make God's law less holy. Let's put the blame where it belongs. The blame has to be put on *hamartia* (sin).

All of this is a biblical pastische. It is about Genesis, says Stanislas Lyonnet, the French Jesuit who sorted this out the best of all the exegetes.[7] He really looked at the text, unlike the mighty articles written by Continental theologians who were influenced by Augustine and who asked, "Who is the I? Is this the 'I' before or after Paul became a Christian? Or is this 'I' in some deeper anthropological sense?" Instead of this line of thought, Lyonnet simply looked and said, "Of course, Paul is preaching a little sermon on Genesis 3, and out of that he gets his answer to the question: "No, the law is holy. But Satan, the dirty double crosser, sure can use it to trick us." And so Paul says, "I was tricked by Satan's command, and so death came into my world as it had to Eve and Adam."

Romans 7:12ff. is one of the most successful chapters in the Bible because it says something psychological: "If I don't act as I want to act, the bad things I do not want to do I do, and the good things I want to do, I don't. Wretched man that I am, who is going to deliver me?" We have all heard those words, and they hit home, don't they? That is pretty much the way it is. The decisive thing is what Paul makes of them. He does not say, "wretched man that I am"—that comes in another context. He says, "I don't understand that I act as I act. The bad things I do not want to do,

I do, and the good things I want to do, I don't. So I agree with the law that it is good." That is what Paul makes of them. "I rejoice in the law. I, with my true ego, serve the law of God. But in the flesh is the law of sin." He can even say, "If I do the things which I do not want to do, it isn't I who do them."

A modern and not so Christian psychology teaches that we are not really responsible for our actions. There is certainly no morose feeling of guilt in this chapter. The feeling is one of tragedy, of realization that dirty sin has mixed into the system, but there is no feeling of guilt whatsoever. How has the tradition been able to read that in, when Paul says so clearly, "I rejoice, I agree with the law"? Actually, Paul's point here is that we are on God's side. We recognize that we gain our proper ego (*autos ego* in verse 25), and we stand on God's side. Let the blame fall where it should fall, namely on sin, and not on me.

This is extremely important for Paul, because for him this sin that rules the world, this sand that has gotten into the machinery, is tragic. The *talaiporos ego anthropos* is not an existential quiver, or a guilt-ridden cry. When Paul speaks about his weakness, it is tragic. But Paul never feels guilty about being weak. He is weak because Satan is slapping him in the face. Weakness comes from outside. This anthropology is totally different from the one that dominates much of our thinking. Never ever does Paul equate weakness with sin. There is a strange rhetorical overlap between Romans 5 and 7, but that's all: Let's blame dirty, tragic reality—*hamartia.*

The tragedy is very clear. The world is not pretty. But Paul thinks in terms of *hamartia*—and here I lift some concepts from Rudolf Bultmann's analysis of this chapter and from Käsemann's interpretation—as a kind of cosmic power. *Hamartia* is a power. It is not the sum total of our little sinning—or our big sinning. When you see it as a power game in which we get trapped, or nations get trapped, then it takes on a meaning more tragic than a guilt-ridden individual. It is very hard for me to understand Paul's saying, "If I do what I do not want to do, it isn't I who do it." Anyone for whom the question of individual guilt is important would not easily make such a statement without at least counterbalancing it with a statement about responsibility. And the responsibility we have in chapters 1–3 is not the responsibility, really, of guilt experienced in an individual way. It is, rather, a lack of perception. It is blindness rather than guilt. Human beings could have seen. Hence they are accountable.

Guilt language, and the very word "guilt," do not occur in Paul. It is true that if there is a possibility of *kata krima* (condemnation), that presupposes that there is a *krima* for which the individual or the world is held responsible. But to Paul sin is tragic rather than laden with guilt.

Where do we go from here hermeneutically? We could use these passages as starting points, just as Satan used holy writ as a starting point. We could also point to the beginning of chapter 5, where we have the *katalagei.* I am trying to get at Paul's overarching perception, and I am also trying to demonstrate a certain type of exegetical exercise that I do, and that I teach students to go through. If you are dealing with a well-known biblical passage, close your eyes or look away from the text and retell the passage to yourself before you read it again. Then see if there is anything a little "off" about your retelling. Usually something in the text will be a little different, if you have keen eyes, from the way you remembered it. Presumably that difference is where you should insert your exegetical can opener.

How can Paul say, "If that's the way it is, it is not I who do it"? How can he say, "I agree with the law"? How can *that* be the point of the text, rather than just getting an existential shiver from it?

Now there is good news. There is an "out," and this out causes Paul to pile up genitives upon genitives upon genitives. He starts to get high—perhaps, also, he doesn't have his thoughts quite clear. But the effect of the prose is overwhelming. "And so there is no condemnation for those who are in Christ Jesus, for the law of the Spirit, of the life in Christ Jesus, has set us free from the law of sin and the law of death. For God has done that which was impossible for the law, since it had been weakened by the flesh." In other words, the medicine was all right. In some sense the law was a power toward health, but, given a certain taintedness of the *sarx*, the flesh, it had the opposite effect. The flesh weakened the law, says Paul. Therefore God sent his own child in the likeness of the flesh of sin, and for sin's sake, and so he condemned the sin that is in the flesh in order that the just requirement of the law be fulfilled in us, who do not walk around according to the flesh but according to the Spirit.

This is the introduction to Paul's "spirit" chapter, and he doesn't expand on it. He is just aware of the fact that here, now, something has come. He soars awfully high on the Spirit, and he even uses the idea of deification or divinization—that the Holy Spirit is in us, and thereby we are of God's quality. Paul escalates one rung after another to a marvelous statement about the spirit in which we cry "Abba, Father." For Paul that word meant inheritance.

"If we say 'Abba, Father,' we are children, and if we are children we are heirs of God and heirs with Christ." First comes the typical Pauline break. "We are heirs if we co-suffer." Then, suddenly, comes the typical Pauline fear—what I call fear of John or Johannine theology, that is to say, fear of a stance of faith where one could say that those who believe have already transferred from death to life, that "one who believes in me will never ever see death." We bend faith over matter; by seeing it, by knowing it, by believing it we have eternal life. But Paul says, "Not so fast. We have a long way to go, and in our present situation we are groaning with the creation." He escalates the weakness motif, and he even says, "Remember that faith is not seen. Faith is only a hope, and a hope that one sees fulfilled is not a hope anymore. We are so weak that we don't even know what to pray, but the Holy Spirit comes and takes us under the arms, lifts us up, and intercedes for us, and speaks in us with unspeakable groans," which is Paul's reference to his *glossolalia.*

Ernst Käsemann is quite right that the phrase "unspeakable groans" means glossolalia. For Paul, unspeakable groans are not a sign of having taken the honors course in the Christian faith, but rather a sign of our weakness. (We can see how he handles the same theme in 1 Corinthians.) But here he has no problem with glossolalia; he is just using it in his own language as an example: "And the one who knows the Spirit which is God can hear what the Spirit prays."

Glossolalia is, in a certain sense, a universal human experience and a very seminal phenomenon in all kinds of religious traditions. But I don't think Paul thought in those terms. He thought that having spoken about the groaning of the creation made the groaning and inarticulateness of glossolalia equal clear speech and knowing what one should pray. He does not say that they are the same. I have read Gerardus van der Leeuw's *Religion in Essence and Manifestation,* and hence I equate these. But Paul read the inarticulateness of glossolalia as a sign of imperfection. The Holy Spirit understands, and God, being Spirit, knows—that is exactly how Paul thinks in 1 Corinthians 14. He views inarticulateness as the characteristic of glossolalia. He has nothing to do with the image of glossolalia in Acts 2, where Luke used it in a symbolic way for languages being heard—a totally different concept.

Not only is the switch in Romans 8 theological—Paul always had a theology of the cross—but Paul never says that we are saved. We have died with Christ, and we shall die with Christ. At most we walk in a spirit of newness, but the consummation and salvation are always in the future. That is one of the marks of the truly Pauline epistles.

aren't saved NOW but rather will be in the future

In Romans 8 Paul had started to present to the Romans his mission and his ministry. In explaining it he had shown how he read God's actions in the world—how he understood the mystery of sin, and how even the holy law of God got tainted. Now the Spirit is bubbling around us and in us, and Paul is on the way back down from his high. He begins to speak about suffering, because that was exactly how he spoke about his weakness when he discussed it in relation to his ministry in the Corinthian correspondence.

The weakness of Paul is a strength, but woe unto you if you think too much about that. The weakness of Paul is also a weakness, and it is experienced as nothing but weakness. Only in the glory of God is there a little transubstantiation.

In Romans 8:31 Paul writes, "What shall we then say to all these things? If God is for us, who can be against us?" This whole section, from verse 31 to 40, comes close to being an exact statement about Paul's ministry. In Corinthians he spoke about all his difficulties and hardships, and of course he had been in more shipwrecks than anybody, and had been beaten and in prison, and on and on. That is the raw material of what is here in Romans.

This is not a description of Christian existence in general; it is like 2 Corinthians 11 and other similar writings. Hardships were pressing in on Paul, as were all kinds of deprivations, including nakedness. "And for your sake we are in the process of dying the whole day." This is Paul, and this is his understanding of his ministry.

4
Missiological Reflections by a Former Zealot: Romans 9–11

Paul says he wants to go to hell at the beginning of Romans 9. He even wants to be *anathema* to Christ if that would help his fellow Jews. He goes on at length, piling up strong language—"I swear," "God is my witness," and so on. Why this intensity? It could be Paul might have given the impression that he didn't really care for Israel of old. "I speak the truth in Christ, I do not lie." His conscience bears witness in the Holy Spirit that there is great sorrow and continuous pangs in his heart. In biblical language the heart is not where we feel, but where we think. Those good old people felt with their guts, and they thought with their hearts. The more Greek we got, the more we emptied the heart of thinking and placed it up in the head. But here Paul certainly thinks and feels and worries with his mind.

Paul used rather strong language of a similar kind at the beginning of the epistle (Romans 1:9), where he called God and the Spirit to witness that he cared for and had wanted all the time to come to the people in Rome. But in chapter 9 he escalated the language, and returned to it in the beginning of chapter 10. It is my *eudokia,* my positive will toward salvation, he says, and his prayer to God is that the Jews come *eis soterian,* that is, that they come toward salvation.

Sometimes I wonder whether this phrasing is what we call *captatio benevolentiae*—a good way to catch the ear of the audience, as if Paul said, "I feel with you an enormous desire, that those who so far have been rather cool to the gospel will come around." But before Paul is through, in Romans 9–11 he actually lectures the Gentiles in Rome, whether he thinks of the Roman congregation primarily as Gentile, or of the Gentiles in the congregation. He addresses them. He says specifically in 11:13, "I speak to you Gentiles." He lectures them on the fact that they are newcomers, that they should stand in awe, that the Jews are in the hands of God, and, as I read it, that it is none of their business to try to manipulate or perhaps even evangelize the Jewish people—"I tell you a mystery lest you be conceited." Paul considers the Gentiles to be potentially and actually conceited in their attitude toward Israel.

At the start one can read this section as Paul identifying with Gentile Christians at the start, but at the end as Paul warning Gentile Christians about overstepping what might be God's plan. If I were to psychologize, and if I were to depend too much on the Book of Acts, I would ask why Paul, this super-missionary, teaches about the limits to missions. Could it be that he had been burned once? That he knew the pitfalls of religious zeal? He knew that somehow there is an instinct in people to think, "The only way God's will can happen is when others become like me." Is that what Romans 9–11 is about?

Paul begins by saying that these fellow Jews of his *kata sarka* (he uses this in the neutral sense, just as he said Jesus was the son of David *kata sarka*) are Israelites; theirs are the sonship, the glory, the covenants, the law, the true worship, the promises, and the fathers out of whom Christ comes according to genealogy. Then he expands his Abraham model. He uses the word *logizestai* again here. (In verse 8, for example, God has a peculiar way of reckoning, Paul says.) The promise manifests itself not as an evergrowing transnational corporation engulfing the world. Rather, it manifests itself in a narrowing way, and Paul lists the whole story: there is Isaac, Rebecca, Jacob and Esau, and there is the peculiar way God used Pharoah to advance his plan. The passage is a study in the way God works. (Compare Steven's speech in Acts 7; one does theology by retelling history with a slant, from a specific angle.)

Paul found this story to be according to the law, according to Torah. It is amazing to what extent his examples in Galatians and especially Romans come exactly from the *nomos*, from the law, from the Torah. He takes joy in proving his point about the law by quoting the law, and that is not accidental. He shows in verse 30 that what actually has come out of this strange history is that the Gentiles (*ethne*) who pursued righteousness found it. They received it. That was the righteousness of faith, Abraham's type of faith, before circumcision. But Israel, pursuing the law, did not arrive at the total, new "rightness" that was in the law. Why? Because they stumbled on that stumbling block God had placed, which was the Christ. Paul's thinking is simple and straightforward. He sees the point he is making as a prefigured and predicted biblical process. That is how God works.

The Jews did not arrive at this *dikaiosyne* (righteousness), because they sought their own—*zetountes ten idian dikaiosynen* (10:3)—not their own in the sense of the one we have in our hearts when we try to be good, but their own in the sense of a righteousness according to the commandments rather than righteousness of faith, which for Paul is a catchword for salvation in Jesus Christ.

Then Paul describes the spirit of these various righteousnesses. He says in 10:5 that Moses writes concerning the righteousness of the law that he who does the right thing shall live by it. To explain the righteousness of faith, in verses 6–9 Paul uses a rather intriguing quotation from Deuteronomy 30:11–14: "But the righteousness based on faith says, Do not say in your heart, 'Who will ascend into heaven?' (that is, to bring Christ down) or 'Who will descend into the abyss?' (that is, to bring Christ up from the dead)." Hence what is needed is the proclamation of this message and its embrace by confessing with one's mouth and believing in one's heart that God raised Jesus from the dead. Up to this point Paul has just been saying what he had already said, fleshing it out, and enlarging it.

Presumably Paul is marvelling in his special calling, the coming of the Gentiles. That is a real mystery to Paul. As a good Jew he is finding, to his amazement—as Christians have done through the ages—that in the very text that comes to us through tradition lies the very truth that criticizes that tradition. That is the spirit of the Reformation, and the spirit of the ongoing, marvelling capacity of the history of interpretation. Playing partly on midrash and on methods of exegesis, Paul proves that the very law he has received as a Jew is the very law that speaks about the way God works, and that has now led to what is for Paul a *fait accompli*—the coming of the Gentile age and the incorporation of the Gentiles. All his quotations circle around that fact, and only in that fact do they have their common denominator.

In the beginning of Romans 11, it is important for Paul that not only he but also others accept this new dispensation, this new *diatheke*. The others are the Jewish Christians, and they are likened unto those who did not bow down to Ba'al in the time of Elijah. Actually, in 11:5 Paul uses (for the only time in the New Testament, I believe) the famous idea of the remnant, "a remnant shall return"—the Jeremiah motif.

I have always been struck by the fact that Christians have not picked up more on this motif. It is really such a natural term for what happens when Jesus comes. The remnant has been an important concept at various stages in history, especially in radical reformation movements. We are those who did not bow down for Ba'al; we are the mysterious remnant, established miraculously and wonderfully by the mighty faith of our fathers. The reason we have so little "remnant theology" in the New Testament is that basically the New Testament is a Gentile Christian book. And remnant language applies in an immediate way to a thinking from within the people of Israel. It is as though Paul said, "In order to move on, God doesn't need more than a remnant. And that remnant enters into holy history."

Then comes the question, "So I ask, did they [namely the Jews] stumble in order to fall (*eptaisan hina pesosin*)?" *Hina* is a tricky work in Greek. Some scholar has even written an article on it typical of our trade: "The Conjunction *Hina* as the Key to the Whole Understanding of Pauline Theology." The Hebrew word is *lema'an*. It really means "in order to." But for some reason it is often used in biblical Greek, more so than in classical Greek, when we really would describe an outcome. Paul sees purpose where we see outcome. The language is actually not Pauline. It is Septuagintal, it is Hebrew, and it offers a wonderful way of seeing the world. What we see as cause and effect, the Greek and the Hebrew see as push and purpose. Everything has this kind of "in order to."

"Did they stumble so as to fall?" No, says Paul, but by their transgression there is salvation for the Gentiles. That is a very simple, basic thought, in one way. Had the Jews not said "no," we would not have the opportunity to get in on the deal. That is why Paul uses the term *paidagogos*, not to mean a teacher, but to mean a kind of guardian, the kind who sees to it that the children do not get into trouble on the way to school, if you will. Paul says that the law has functioned as a guardian or "babysitter" for Israel, so that Israel does not raid the icebox before the big party comes around. God has decided that the big party must wait until the Gentiles can also come. So the law served as a *paidagogos*, a watchdog, for Israel, until the coming of the Christ and the Gentiles.

This is the basic Pauline speculation, but in Romans 11 Paul unexpectedly turns the idea another way. "Their stumbling is your glory," he writes. This pattern of thought has been historicized by Luke. In the Book of Acts, Paul always goes first to the synagogue to register the "no" of the Jews, so that he has the liberty, the right, to go to the Gentiles. This is a theological concept, not a missionary strategy in the practical sense, because Luke repeats that statement that nothing really came of it—a couple of women, but in Paul's view, that did not even add up to a minion. So the method isn't effective. On the contrary, registering the "no" of the Jews gives Paul the license to turn to the Gentiles.

Paul addresses those Gentiles (*hymin gar lego tois ethnesin*) in verse 13. "It it to you Gentiles I speak," he says, and he reminds them that they are newcomers. They have been engrafted. Paul was from the city, so he did not really understand how grafting works. The image is the reverse of what really happens. Grafting is done to revive an old tree. But, nevertheless, Paul uses the image for his argument here.

Paul is thinking about the question of what this whole history suggests for a Gentile attitude toward the Jews. He perceives in the Gentile community a quite obvious haughtiness, a conceit, a lack of concern that he is trying to combat. If that is the case, Paul's intensity in those first words of Romans 9 could mean, "I am going to show them that a true Christian really is deeply concerned about the people of Israel. I swear that I am so concerned that if it would help that I were *anathema* to Christ, I would take that road."

Paul was not anti-Semitic. He is actually the only one in the early church who recognized the necessity of correcting condescending attitudes toward the Jewish people. That is what Paul sets out to do in Romans 9–11. But, of course, his patterns of thinking—especially when one takes them out of context or misinterprets his warning—have fed into all kinds of anti-Semitism. Paul is saying what the Jews have always said—"The kingdom hasn't come yet. You have the law, but you don't really live by it." That is the main criticism of Christianity by Jews when they say, "You claim that the kingdom has come, but it doesn't look that way." Paul says to the Jews, "The kingdom hasn't come, but I announce that it is available in Jesus Christ." He is not doing anti-Semitic work. He is making the usual Jewish argument that we live in a world of imperfection. But then Paul turns the argument on them, just as he does with Moses.

Since the kingdom did not come, but the Christians had the king, they stopped speaking about the kingdom and started to speak about the king. Jesus spoke about the kingdom, but Christians spoke about Jesus. Why? Because the kingdom hadn't come. Christ became the answer to that embarrassing fact. That is why kingdom language dies; it is practically nonexistent outside of the Gospels. There is very little kingdom language even in the Book of Acts written by Luke, and its absence there is stunning, if the same person is doing all the writing or speaking. The fact that attention moved to the king has had all kinds of consequences for Christian history.

While Paul is not speaking about the kingdom in Romans, he does turn the perspective and the hermeneutical center back to the question of what God is doing in the world, which is close to the kingdom issue. We always think we must first get the right relation to God, and then, by means of what German Lutherans call *die quellende Liebe* (love that gushes forth), if we just have the right relation to God, if we simply pull the lever, like the slot machines of Las Vegas, the cash will fall out. But that is not how Paul sees the world. Paul sees the world as acted upon by God, and he tries to understand where we are in God's mysteries.

How are Jews and Gentiles to relate? How are Gentiles to think? In 11:20 Paul says they had better not think haughtily (*me hypsela phronein*). He gives the Romans a picture of Gentiles as honorary Jews. Christians, when they are very generous, might even consider making a Jew an honorary Christian. Paul, however, turned the tables.

In 11:25 come Paul's famous words: "For I do not want you to be ignorant of this mystery, lest you be conceited" (*en heautois phronimoi*). Israel is "sort of" (*apo merous*) under a cloud, to be sure. I find that *apo merous* can best be translated into colloquial English as "sort of." Paul used this term often. In Romans 15:15 he says, for example, "I have written boldly to you, sort of." The whole of Israel will be saved. He doesn't say Israel will accept Jesus Christ. Since Romans 10:17, or in some manuscripts since 10:9, Paul has not mentioned the name Jesus or Christ. This is one of the few extended theological arguments Paul carries on in pure God-language, not in christological language. At the end he writes his only doxology in pure God-language, without a christological note. He may have done it on purpose. Perhaps he didn't want Christians to have a "Christ-flag" to wave. Here he spoke only God-language, which is rare in Paul.

Yet in a certain sense Paul always spoke God-language. He seldom says that Christ has risen, but, rather, that God raised Christ. In the classical liturgy of the Eucharist we do not pray to Christ. We pray to God, and speak about Christ in the third person. Perhaps this way of being directed toward God is not so rare in Paul, since he never prays to Christ. He can argue with Christ, perhaps, about his mission in 2 Corinthians, but his prayers are always to God. In Romans he is speaking God-language throughout, and the doxology at the end of chapter 11 is directed to the mysteries of God. It may be conscious, or perhaps it is unconscious, and that makes it even more interesting.

To be able to think about this question of the Jews without mentioning the name of Christ is the sin of sins in most Christian circles. But you can't really accuse Paul of being afraid to mention the name of Christ when it is right to mention it. He was not ashamed of the gospel. All his letters make that very clear.

Romans discusses the desirable Gentile attitude and, at the beginning of chapter 11, the letter takes up the subject of Peter as the apostle to the circumcised. There are Jews who have accepted Jesus Christ, and Paul sees Jewish Christians as the remnant. But why is Paul so overtly non-christological at exactly this point and so unlike the rest of the epistles?

One has the right to use Paul's hesitation as a key to rethinking missions in general, and my argument is very simple. Paul shatters universalism—"the only way people can be saved is to become like me, and if they are not like me, I pronounce them to be like me"—which is the climax of Christian condescension. God is not trying to run the world like a corporation, expanding its market at any price. People will say, "But there is something peculiar about the people of Israel." Of course there is; there is something peculiar about every people. The whole epistle to the Romans, not only chapters 9–11, is of enormous importance to any discussion of how one can sing one's song to Jesus without telling disparaging stories about others.

If I were to tell a story based on a New Testament text of Paul's, but in the fashion of the rabbis, I would think about those words that got Origen into trouble: "There are many things that have to happen first, but finally all will be in Christ's hands, and Christ will lay it down before God, and God will become all in all" (1 Cor. 15:28 and the preceding verses). I would expound on that notion by saying that it is Judgment Day. We Lutherans are up front, and as we look around, others are also there—not only other Christians, but Hindus, Buddhists, Jews, everybody, and it is wonderful. It is just as we thought. Here is God, and here is Christ on the right hand. Heaven is a cathedral for those who like cathedrals, and it is a wonderful forest for those who like to worship nature. As far as God and Christ are concerned, they are exactly as we were taught. Then we then turn to those around us with a slightly supercilious smile that says: "Isn't it wonderful that you are here, too; as you see, it is as I said—with Christ." But when we turn back toward God, there is no Christ to be seen, because Christ is never present to feed into the smugness of his followers. That is the ultimate *theologia crucis,* and there is something of it in the God-language of Romans.

Instead of speaking about Jesus in Romans 11:26, Paul says something mysterious—"For it is out of Zion that the rescuer will come." We Christians read that immediately as a reference to Jesus. But it could just as well be read as a Pauline form of the famous statement in the Gospel of John (4:22), when Jesus says to the Samaritan woman, "For salvation is from the Jews"—that those who were in are out, and those who were out are in. God is running this strange show, to which Paul can only say, "The Jews are in the hands of God and at the mercy of God, and the promises of God are irreversible. God does not go back on his promises. God might repent of his plans of judgment, but he never repents of his plans of mercy." (Compare this to the wonderful repentance of God in the Book of Jonah.)

Paul says, "The Jews are in God's hands. The only thing you have to do is be faithful, and this is a mystery." In other words, "Get off the backs of the Jews, and leave them in the hands of God." God has the power to realize their salvation, which is definitely not cast in christological terms. In Romans Paul is speaking to the Gentiles, not to the church; in Galatians he is speaking about both.

The expression "the whole of Israel," in my judgment, stands over against those who had not bowed down to Ba'al. There was the remnant, and there was the whole of Israel. This is not the church being called Israel, or some other kind of inclusiveness. I believe that the word *Israel* is never used in the New Testament about the church. The classic passage is Galatians 6:16: "And as many as walk according to these standards, peace upon them and mercy, and upon the Israel of God." I read this to mean, "and mercy *also* upon the Israel of God." You really cannot read it any other way. Even in the letter to the Galatians, Paul is praying for mercy on the Israel of God, the old Israel. But of course we have appropriated it for ourselves.

A few notes now on hermeneutics, or, in simple language, "so what?" We have raised the question, "What might we think that Paul thought he thought?" That is what I call the "then" meaning. To do that is to feel like a tree-surgeon who cuts back radically on the tree. I have no illusions that the good old homiletical habits will sprout up among us all. But it is helpful to cut it back, to adopt a minimalist point of view, to find the anvil on which Paul hammered out these words and thoughts, and to see their function. That's what *Sitz im Leben* means. *Sitz im Leben* presupposes the place and function of the text in the life of the church. Was it for encouragement? Was it for *paranesis?* Was it a doxology to be sung as a hymn? The *Sitz im Leben* of Paul's Epistle to the Romans is Paul's mission within God's total plan. Hence the epistle deals with Jews and Gentiles.

Paul teaches in one way or another that ultimately the Jews—or Israel—are going to be saved. If you asked, "But what about those Jews who died before the time?" Paul would not understand your question. It would be meaningless. That's not what he was speaking about. He was speaking about the grand plan of God and his humble yet important role within it. From a hermeneutical point of view, the primary application of Paul's letter to the Romans is to understand the strange ways of God and the mission of the church. *It is missiology, not soteriology.* Romans is a tractate on mission, not just in terms of outreach, but in terms of how Paul's bringing the message to the Gentiles fits into God's total plan.

That primary application is not irrelevant to us today. One of the more important tasks for the church at this time is to understand its mission rightly. We are still learning about relations between Jews and Christians. Perhaps we should allow ourselves to use Paul's warnings and his way of thinking about how God acts as a guide to the rather tough problem of the right mission stance for the Christian community. Missiology is going through tremendous soul-searching, to the point that one finds it almost impossible to disentangle Western imperialism from the Christian gospel. We can understand a vote in Africa for a moratorium on missions. We understand why our sisters and brothers in the African churches say to us "Get off our backs, because you do more harm than good despite your good intentions."

Missiologists would be well-advised to consider the way Paul thinks about his mission. He understands that God does not work in a straight line, and that straight-line theology always leads to conceit. Paul, the great missionary, warns the Gentiles about the mission to the Jews. He sees that it is the plan of God for the Jesus movement to become a Gentile movement.

The whole question of universalism and particularism and missions is a major subject for the contemporary Western church. If we start to look at missions as Paul looked at Israel and the Gentile church—as two minorities whose witnesses were somehow necessary to God's mysterious dealings with the world, then we have recovered the biblical perspective. Just as Israel was meant to be a light to the Gentiles, so Jesus spoke about his disciples as a light unto the world. Light and salt are minority images. Jesus did not say, "Let your light so shine before people that they see your good deeds and become Christians." He said, "that they see your good deeds and praise your Father who is in heaven." This is the Jewish way of speaking. Do not think that the salvation of the world means that people should become like us, but that somehow God needs our witness as a catalyst in the sea of humankind.

In Judaism this idea received perhaps its clearest theological expression in Leo Baeck, though not in his later work. Baeck began his teaching and his rabbinate in Germany, and then came to the United States. One can find in his writing an extremely moving expression of the acceptance of the diaspora cast in liberal terms. The diaspora is not only acceptable, but it is a meaningful way for Israel to be. Critics would say this view represents the usual "making a virtue out of necessity." But there is a rich tradition behind it. I think, for instance, of Hungary, where I visited the Jewish community and was given marvelous examples of the weight of rabbinic tradition. Hungarian Jews would say, "It is the will of God that we are the nation without a land, and hence the hardship of our dispersion has proven a gift to the world and to us."

That is not the whole reality of Judaism, of course, but it is one strand in the Jewish tradition. The whole motif of being a light unto the nations, and the awareness that Israel has a weighty, glorious burden to bear, having been called by God to be a holy people, has never meant that God is only the God of the Jews. It is a pluralistic model. That is why we also have this image of being a light unto the nations in the teachings of Jesus. It comes in the discussion of the blessing of all by Abraham, which Paul related especially to the notion that in *Christ* Israel becomes a blessing to humankind. This narrowing down to Jesus Christ is a Christian interpretation, but the image has a more general meaning. As Paul said, the Jews have the *hyothesia*—the status of children. They do not need to come to Christ in order to be children of God. Because they have the *hyothesia*, they live in the world as a light. "It is too little for you just to be something for the people of Israel," we read in Isaiah 49:6. That theme is picked up in the Song of Simeon in Luke 2—"a light for revelation to the Gentiles." But we should not forget that Simeon's song also says, "and for glory to your people Israel."

Not until after Constantine did Christians get the itch to conquer the world for Christ. They thought of themselves as a peculiar people, as a light and as salt, witnessing and letting the chips fall where they may. God, miraculously, needed this witness. Think about the Magi. The Bible does not say that they started a church when they got home. But they got the lift of their lives from their journey. They saw and rejoiced in the light, and they praised God.

There are two ways of thinking about God. One way is to imagine a God who asks, first thing every morning, "What are the statistics on the saved?"

Another is to have a God who asks, first thing, "Has there been any progress for the kingdom?" These are two distinct theologies. Paul's theology was the latter. He saw the mystery of God's workings not as a kind of universalism, but as the faithfulness of a new witnessing people, a witness now based on Jesus Christ and knowing no particular race or sex.

That is the image in Romans, and it deals with our problems. We can manicure our own souls only so long. When it comes to the epistle to the Romans, the enormous preoccupation with our egos that is part of our tradition moves the topic of the epistle away not only from God's way of dealing with the world, but also from the missionary task of the church, and into the private realm of our sin and guilt. Such a preoccupation also overlooks what I suggested in relation to Romans 6 where Paul says that macro models do not always work well for micro problems. The tradition of interpreting Romans—even Luther's enormous insights, which were great gospel to manic depressive people like himself—does just the opposite of what Paul was doing in Romans. It makes us turn inward *(incurvatus in se,* as Luther expressed it) and become preoccupied with ourselves. That was not the intention. By centering the problem in the question of individual salvation, we forget what the letter was about.

The Asian scholar Choan Seng Song has written an article on the subject of many languages and many peoples.[8] His famous reinterpretation of the Tower of Babel explains the story in terms of the fear of people at being dispersed, the fear of pluralism. It is a ferocious critique of the theological effects of the history of salvation, and of the tendency we Westerners have to think that wherever we go, we lift people into history. (But here I must note a new Swedish translation of the Bible—the first Bible I have seen that includes a map of China.)

The point of hermeneutics is to say, "Not so fast, sisters and brothers." The density of biblical authority is heaviest when the analogy is closest. The more footwork we do, and the further away the analogy gets, the more the authority of the Scriptures diminishes. We cannot be so sure that we are on the right track. If we start to read Romans as a letter about how God might think about the world and the role of our common life and witness in it, and about universalism, it sounds beautiful. But universalism is always the root of imperialism. If you are a universalist, then your way of thinking, by necessity, must be right for everybody, especially if your basic model of salvation is victory coming out of the Exodus. If you combine the victory model with the universalist model, you just cannot avoid crusades.

If there is real universalism, and you know what is right, then woe unto those who do not think likewise.

By contrast, there was the wonderful particularism of Israel, which wanted to be, and will one day be again, a light unto the nations. Israel has capacities within itself for that, we know. Although Israel thought of itself as a light unto the nations, it never had the idea that the only way for God to accomplish that was to make everybody a Jew. We usually downgrade particularism. We are universalists, as was the Hellenistic culture that forced itself on the world and that led, among other things, to the Maccabean revolt. There is a wisdom in particularism, in being peculiar and letting your light shine or your little lamp flicker, in being a presence that leaves the results to God.

Paul feeds into all these themes when he speaks about how he tries to reckon the way God works. Paul always knows he is right. When he is unbearable in all respects, he is always right. And yet he knows that there is a limit. The Jewish scholar David Hartman has written a new model of theology in which he says: salvation is the recognition of limits. We think of fullness as blowing ourselves up to be bigger and bigger. But fullness can only be had by shrinking enough to recognize the other, who makes us full, and that is also true of our relation to God.

Paul argues, in his own way, within this whole realm. Therein lies the importance and relevance of what he says. Unless we recognize limits, we will not come back to that healthy image of God who is concerned about the kingdom.

God will always find enough people to carry the torch, if we can get over the idea so totally absent from Romans that salvation means we win and others become like unto ourselves. And Paul's perspective on salvation comes from one of the most committed missionaries the church honors in its memory.

5
Intellectual Worship and Respect for Conviction: Romans 12–14

Once theologians have a great theological thought, they always feel that before they are through, they also have to squeeze ethics out of it. If you have a great insight, as Paul had about justification by faith, woe unto you unless you prove its truth by showing that without that *right* concept, you can never act as an ethical being.

Before Paul is through, he gives ethical admonitions to the church in Rome. Of course he is in some trouble, since he had said that he had no right to admonish the Romans. So he introduces his admonitions with a beautiful phrase: "I admonish you brothers and sisters in Christ, through the compassion of God," followed by something of an anthology of his thoughts from elsewhere in his letters, not unlike the preacher who lifts a thought from one sermon to another. Paul had given much oral and written *parenesis* to his churches, and large segments of what comes in Romans 12–14 had been worked out in Corinth, or other similar situations. Theology and preaching are like frog eggs. It is very hard to get just one egg. They all hang together. Paul gets into certain themes, and it all flows as he speaks. Here, in 12–14, he is going to "do ethics." But perhaps one should point out that Christian existence does not a Christian ethic make. It is, rather, a license as well as a chosen sensibility, by which we both use and learn from ethical systems. There are no Christian ethics, but there might be Christian sensitivities to ethical issues.

I have stressed a macro-micro dichotomy to show that Paul's way of thinking about big things is not the model he used when he thought about how one should behave or live. There is a certain disconnection between Paul's theological and ethical thinking that I want to demonstrate. It is strange to behold, since Paul does not know too much about the Roman congregation. I am familiar with this phenomenon from the preachers who are invited to Harvard University. Only two Bible texts come to their minds, and we hear them constantly from visiting preachers. If they are liberal we will hear that "the truth shall make you free," since the word on the Harvard seal is *veritas.* If they are a little more evangelical, the sermon text will be 1 Corinthians 1: "The Greeks desire wisdom, but I preach a crucified Lord." Why do we hear so many such sermons at Harvard? Because these images suggest themselves to preachers when they think about what Harvard stands for.

I suggest that Paul is thinking about Rome in a similar way, and it gives him a little shiver. He is trying to write at the proper cultural and educational level. He starts off, actually, with something that comes very naturally to Stoic philosophy. He speaks about giving our whole lives as a living sacrifice, which was a slogan in Jewish terminology. The living sacrifice was a critique of polytheism. And this living, acceptable sacrifice is going to be the *logike latreia,* a word that has been translated in many different ways. The King James Version speaks about our "reasonable worship." But more recent translations have moved more and more to our "spiritual service." When we do not know what something actually means, we can always spiritualize. There is some slight evidence for giving it that meaning. But what is the opposite of "spiritual service"? Is it the kind of worship where one really does something—really makes offerings pleasing to the gods? Or is it a service that is unaware of God as spirit? The New English Bible says, "worship offered by mind and heart," which is not bad. Actually, *latreia* means worship, so "service" is correct in that sense. It can also mean "for such is the worship that you as rational creatures should offer." That is a modern way of saying "reasonable." In 1611 reasonable meant rational, and rational is the correct translation. We find the best example of this word and its meaning in Epictetus, who used *logikos* to say that we praise God according to our nature as rational human beings.

In the passage that follows, there is, more than in any other passage in Paul that I know, an abundance of words for the mind, for thinking, for what we would call "brain activities." Rational beings who do not conform to this age but who are transformed in their *nous,* their mind, can figure out or approve or discern what is good, what is acceptable, what is perfect, what is the will of God. That is the tone that Paul is setting in what follows: Let's think straight. "Transformed in our minds" does not mean that we should not use our minds. They are renewed minds. We don't hear this so much in some translations because, sadly, we are not much for the mind in the church. Heart language is always closer to the church. No one ever really says that you have to sharpen your brain in Jesus' name. It is always the heart, and that is not good.

In Romans Paul is constantly saying, "It is a matter of thinking." In 12:3, "Do not think more highly than you have reason to think," but *eis to sophronein*—think with sober thinking, or wise thinking, or sober estimate, "according to the measure of faith that God has meted out." In verses 16 and 17, the thinking language has been smuggled out of most translations—*auto eis allelous phronountes*—"thinking the same in relation to one another." What matters is not how we *feel* about others, but how we *think* about them. "Don't think haughty things"—*ta hypsela*—Paul says in verse 16. Paul's "brain" language is striking. When he comes to ethics he does not say, "now we have learned about justification by faith," or "now we have learned about the big schemes of God, and from that follows...since of course theology should pay off."

No, Paul shifts, as he does so often. When he deals with ethics, he seems to ask, "What is the best model, the best image, the best argument?" That was precisely what he did when he had trouble in Corinth. He built his whole argument on the image of planting when he spoke about the various factions there. "Apollos watered, but I laid the foundation" (Paul's usual humility), but he also said, "this is not a fight between different philosophies. You do not understand the mysteries of the church if you think of it as a competition between various theologies, as the philosophical schools are fighting. No, we are building an *oikodomé*. We are a garden, a planting." Paul consciously used images that were appropriate to his ethical, ecumenical thought.

Then Paul came up against the problem of those who were haughty in their *gnosis*, and he observes that *gnosis*, knowledge, puffs up but love builds up (1 Cor. 8:1). That leads to the hymn to love in chapter 13. He didn't think at all that this *agape* had anything to do with God's *agape*. I always find it strange that people use this text at weddings, for it is, of course, about the competition of gifts in the church at Corinth. It is an argument for solving the tensions in the community. We can detect no awareness whatsoever in Paul's mind that this text had anything to do with Anders Nygren's *agape* of God, either. Paul just grabbed the metaphor he needed. He did not have to connect it to a specific, preceding, systematic theological thought.

Knowledge puffs up, and love builds up, and Paul is not using that language in order to say that there is much love in the church. On the contrary, he said, if you are going to be a church, and if you are going to be able to stand such distressing fellow Christians as we Christians often are to one another, and as we find others to be, you surely need love. Love is measured by the amount of tension it can take, not by how it feels.

The ethics of Romans 13–14 are not deduced out of the theological part of the epistle (1–11). What Paul described there was a rerun lifted up to a more general level, and shortened so that it is somewhat harder to understand the connection. We are familiar with his thinking from 1 Corinthians on the body and the different gifts, the *charismata*, and even his mention of administration as a gift of the spirit in 1 Corinthians 12. We should pray just as much when we administer as when we prepare sermons; they are equally gifts of the spirit. That is Paul's thinking.

In Romans this returns, but it is much more compressed. What is it that holds the unity of the *charismata* together in 1 Corinthians 12–14? It is the Spirit. "You can't say Jesus is Lord except in the Spirit." Thus we all have the Spirit, and the Spirit has different manifestations (*ta charismata tou pneumatos*). But in Romans there is no Spirit. Paul was discussing exactly the same problem, but the Holy Spirit isn't even mentioned. He was trying something else. What holds the church together? There is the body, of course, but how does Paul understand that which holds the body together? The church is organized not by different gifts of the Spirit, but by measures of faith (12:3), and everyone should think (*sophronein*), should have this wise and balanced and sober thinking, according to how God has measured out faith. Instead of having the gifts of one and the same Spirit, Paul now speaks about "thinking according to one's measure of faith."

C. E. B. Cranfield has a long discussion about this "measure of faith."[9] His piety seems to be at stake on this subject, It is almost the only emotional passage in his two volumes. One cannot imagine degrees of faith in Paul, or in good theology, Cranfield says. How could Paul say that there are "measures" of faith, that some have a little and some have much? If there is justification by faith, how can you have measures of faith? Are you then a little more or a little less justified? That does not work. It must mean, "According to that faith that has been equally measured out to all." Everybody has faith, according to Luke 6:38 ("For the measure you give will be the measure you get back"), but Cranfield doesn't make use of that. He turns instead to the verse in the Gospels about "a full measure, shaken down, and well-packed." Of course this is not what Paul meant.

It is often argued convincingly that Paul is organizing the ethics of the church not around the Spirit, which he spoke about in Corinthians, but around the faith principle he has spoken about in Romans. We get faith up and down for eleven chapters in Romans, and then ethics. Suddenly ethics is organized by faith. That seems to fit, but it really doesn't, because here Paul speaks about faith in a drastically different manner. Look at Romans 14:1: "Accept those who are weak with respect to the faith." "Weak" and "strong" are not so different from "measures." They are gradations. It would be an unbearable construction of the Greek to say, "They are not weak, all living in the same faith." But "accept those who are weak in faith, but not for the purpose of argumentation"—that is a marvelous statement. Paul is speaking to the strong here, which no doubt means those who have transcended their need for religious pedantry, those who are not shy about breaking with behavioral patterns as they have come to know them. Paul is lifting the subject up in a more general way because he wants to be clear that he is not lecturing them. On a rather sophisticated level he says: "Some believe so as to eat everything, to be omnivorous, but the weak ones are vegetarians." He goes into various kinds of *schismata* in the church about lifestyle and behavior. Paul is doing something here that he did in Corinth, but with much greater generality. He says that the strong should accept the weak, the other, even if he or she has another lifestyle.

Paul knows that he is right. He counts himself among the strong. His text has nothing to do with the weakness language he uses when he says, "when I am strong I am weak." That had to do with his sickness and was another way of using "weak" and "strong." In Romans, having "measures of faith" and using our gifts "in proportion to our faith" (12:6) means that some have much faith, and some have little. Paul can think that thought. He understands very well that this is so, but the point is that this fact doesn't split the church apart.

Maybe it is strange that there is no reference to *agape* in Romans, while in Corinthians it is the key word to solving some of the same problems, and it was such a good idea in Corinthians. Paul's basic idea there was that love is measured by its capacity to tolerate diversity and tension. We all know that most of us behave better on the job than when we are at home. That is the way it should be, because there has to be some place in the world where we can be ourselves, where we can anticipate sufficient elasticity of love so that we can be as nasty and as ugly as we are. But in Romans Paul doesn't argue that way. He uses another image, and he thinks much more like a philosopher. As human beings with reason we are called upon to "think right"—*logike.* The only thing that really matters is that we are convinced (*plerophoreistho,* 14:5). Get together, Paul says, but not for the purpose of arguing to see whether you can be together. The only thing that matters is that *hekostos en to idio noi,* that each is fully convinced in his own mind. As Catholic ethics holds, you are morally bound to follow your conscience, even if it is contrary to the teachings of the church. You cannot dissimulate.

Paul is groping not for a new thought, but for one that is found only in this epistle. Perhaps his effort was triggered by his idea that when one speaks to Rome, one should show that one has had an honors course at the university. Paul is showing off, I think. That is the key to his thinking here, and he is so dead sure that he is right. In 1 Corinthians he spoke so much about love because he was almost about to be kicked out. He was low on the totem pole. He has to plead to stay in the mix, as one of many. That was the best he could settle for. He needed love; he needed a principle of accepting variety. That was not the case in Galatia, where he was also beleaguered, but at least according to his own perception he could say, "If I shout enough I might still bring them back," and he sure did.

I would say that need for love is true of all of us. We never understand love until we need it. Our claim that we are the loving community, and that our ethical problem is to whom to give our love is the reason Jesus told the story of the Good Samaritan and then asked not, "Who treated the Samaritan as his neighbor?" but "who *became* a neighbor to the Samaritan?"

But in Romans we don't have love language when Paul deals with questions of diversity; we have philosophical thought concerning individual conviction and behavior. This is, of course, the reason our translations of Romans 14:22–23 should cut back, again, on theological depth. The passage says, "You have faith (*pistis*). Keep it to yourself before God. Blessed is the one who does not judge himself. You can approve things without self-condemnation, but the one who has doubts is condemned if acting, since that is not done out of faith. For everything that is not done out of faith is sin."

That is one of the passages that gives theologians goose bumps, especially if you are a good Lutheran. It is dripping with theological potential. "For everything that is not done out of faith is sin." The New English Bible, although wordy, renders it rather well. "If you have a clear conviction, apply it to yourself in the sight of God." I would not say "apply it;" I would say, "that is between you and God." If you have faith, keep it to yourself before God.

"Happy are those who can make their decisions with a clear conscience. But those who have doubts are guilty if they eat, for their action does not arise from their conviction. And anything that does not arise from conviction is sin." Paul's language when he comes to ethics is toned down and totally different from the enormous decibels of the "rock concert" about justification by faith in Romans 1–11. Now Paul is speaking about the *plerephoreistai,* about the importance of not forcing others to act out of guilt as you want them to act. Then they would commit the sin of sins—the sin of not being true to themselves. "For everything that is not done with *conviction* is sin."

I agree with Ernst Käsemann about many passages in Romans, especially those passages where even he cannot dwell on justification by faith. He is a very good exegete, but he does indicate in his introduction to his commentary on Romans that his is not an average commentary. He wrote it with his life's blood. Actually, he fears that unless he insists on justification by faith, the Catholics will win. He really is still fighting the battles of the Reformation on this score, though he recognizes that the church of Rome has changed. Justification by faith is the article by which the church stands or falls—*articulus stantis et cadentis ecclesiae.* So much is at stake for Käsemann, and it is a challenge to discuss these matters with him.[10] But anyone who can construct the world around the law and gospel problematic, as he does, has forgotten to look at the world for a while.

Käsemann has translated Romans 14:22, "Hold fast the faith that you have for yourself in relation to God." That is a monstrosity. A kind of relationship language enters in because, of course, faith is what establishes our relationship to God. Instead of keeping our faith to ourselves before God, and not lording it over others, Käsemann gives us a big theological statement about Christian existence, and goes on to say in verse 23, "for anything that does not take place out of *faith* is sin," which for Käsemann means faith in Christ who justifies the impious and the ungodly.[11]

This is an excellent example of what I have called the disjunction between macro and micro problems. Or call it the freedom of Paul not to be so infatuated with his own theological system that he has to squeeze everything out of it. When he deals with ethics, he can speak like he does near the end of this letter. Paul is not compulsive about the relationship between *kerygma* and *didache,* or law and gospel, or gospel and law—or any of the constructs with which we have cluttered up a simple reading of this hastily written, but deeply felt letter—Paul's letter to the Romans.

Appendix
Paul's Letter to the Romans

CHAPTER 1

Paul, a servant of Jesus Christ, called to be an apostle, set apart for the gospel of God [2]which he promised beforehand through his prophets in the holy scriptures, [3]the gospel concerning his Son, who was descended from David according to the flesh [4]and designated Son of God in power according to the Spirit of holiness, by his resurrection from the dead, Jesus Christ our Lord,[5]through whom we have received grace and apostleship to bring about obedience to the faith for the sake of his name among all the nations, [6]including yourselves who are called to belong to Jesus Christ;

7 To all God's beloved in Rome, who are called to be saints:

Grace to you and peace from God our Father and the Lord Jesus Christ.

8 First, I thank my God through Jesus Christ for all of you, because your faith is proclaimed in all the world.[9]For God is my witness, whom I serve with my spirit in the gospel of his Son, that without ceasing I mention you always in my prayers, [10]asking that somehow by God's will I may now at last succeed in coming to you. [11]For I long to see you, that I may impart to you some spiritual gift to strengthen you, [12]that is, that we may be mutually encouraged by each other's faith, both yours and mine. [13]I want you to know, brethren, that I have often intended to come to you (but thus far have been prevented), in order that I may reap some harvest among you as well as among the rest of the Gentiles. [14]I am under obligation both to Greeks and to barbarians, both to the wise and to the foolish: [15]so I am eager to preach the gospel to you also who are in Rome.

16 For I am not ashamed of the gospel: it is the power of God for salvation to every one who has faith, to the Jew first and also to the Greek.

[17]For in it the righteousness of God is revealed through faith for faith; as it is written, "He who through faith is righteous shall live."

18 For the wrath of God is revealed from heaven against all ungodliness and wickedness of men who by their wickedness suppress the truth. [19]For what can be known about God is plain to them, because God has shown it to them.[20]Ever since the creation of the world his invisible nature, namely, his eternal power and deity, has been clearly perceived in the things that have been made. So they are without excuse;[21]for although they knew God they did not honor him as God or give thanks to him, but they became futile in their thinking and their senseless minds were darkened. [22]Claiming to be wise, they became fools, [23]and exchanged the glory of the immortal God for images resembling mortal man or birds or animals or reptiles.

24 Therefore God gave them up in the lusts of their hearts to impurity, to the dishonoring of their bodies among themselves, [25]because they exchanged the truth about God for a lie and worshiped and served the creature rather than the Creator, who is blessed forever! Amen.

26 For this reason God gave them up to dishonorable passions. Their women exchanged natural relations for unnatural, [27]and the men likewise gave up natural relations with women and were consumed with passion for one another, men committing shameless acts with men and receiving in their own persons the due penalty for their error.

28 And since they did not see fit to acknowledge God, God gave them up to a base mind and to improper conduct. [29]They were filled with all manner of wickedness, evil, covetousness, malice. Full of envy, murder, strife, deceit, malignity, they are gossips, [30]slanderers, haters of God, insolent, haughty, boastful, inventors of evil, disobedient to parents, [31]foolish, faithless, heartless, ruthless. [32]Though they know God's decree that those who do such things deserve to die, they not only do them but approve those who practice them.

CHAPTER 2

Therefore you have no excuse, O man, whoever you are, when you judge another; for in passing judgment upon him you condemn yourself, because you, the judge, are doing the very same things. [2]We know that the judgment of God rightly falls upon those who do such things. [3]Do you suppose, O man, that when you judge those who do such things and yet do them yourself, you will escape the judgment of God? [4]Or do you presume upon the riches of his kindness and forbearance and patience? Do you not know that God's kindness is meant to lead you to repentance? [5]But by your hard and impenitent heart you are storing up wrath for yourself on the day of wrath when God's righteous judgment will be revealed. [6]For he will render to every man according to his works: [7]to those who by patience and well-doing seek for glory and honor and immortality, he will give eternal life; [8]but for those who are factious and do not obey the truth, but obey wickedness, there will be wrath and fury. [9]There will be tribulation and distress for every human being who does evil, the Jew first and also the Greek, [10]but glory and honor and peace for every one who does good, the Jew first and also the Greek. [11]For God shows no partiality.

12 All who have sinned without the law will also perish without the law, and all who have sinned under the law will be judged by the law. [13]For it is not the hearers of the law who are righteous before God, but the doers of the law who will be justified. [14]When Gentiles who have not the law do by nature what the law requires, they are a law to themselves, even though they do not have the law. [15]They show that what the law requires is written on their hearts, while their conscience also bears witness and their conflicting thoughts accuse or perhaps excuse them [16]on that day when, according to my gospel, God judges the secrets of men by Christ Jesus.

17 But if you call yourself a Jew and rely upon the law and boast of your relation to God [18]and know his will and approve what is excellent, because you are instructed in the law, [19]and if you are sure that you are a guide to the blind, a light to those who are in darkness, [20]a corrector of the foolish, a teacher of children, having in the law the embodiment of knowledge and truth— [21]you then who teach others, will you not teach yourself? While you preach against stealing, do you steal? [22]You who say that one must not commit adultery, do you commit adultery? You who abhor idols, do you rob temples? [23]You who boast in the law, do you dishonor God by breaking the law?n[24]For, as it is written, "The name of God is blasphemed among the Gentiles because of you."

25 Circumcision indeed is of value if you obey the law; but if you break the law, your circumcision becomes uncircumcision. [26]So, if a man who is uncircumcised keeps the precepts of the law, will not his uncircumcision be regarded as circumcision? [27]Then those who are physically uncircumcised but keep the law will condemn you who have the written code and circumcision but break the law. [28]For he is not a real Jew who is one outwardly, nor is true circumcision something external and physical. [29]He

is a Jew who is one inwardly, and real circumcision is a matter of the heart, spiritual and not literal. His praise is not from men but from God.

CHAPTER 3

Then what advantage has the Jew? Or what is the value of circumcision? [2]Much in every way. To begin with, the Jews are entrusted with the oracles of God. [3]What if some were unfaithful? Does their faithlessness nullify the faithfulness of God? [4]By no means! Let God be true though every man be false, as it is written,

"That thou mayest be justified in thy words,
and prevail when thou art judged."

[5]But if our wickedness serves to show the justice of God, what shall we say? That God is unjust to inflict wrath on us? (I speak in a human way.) [6]By no means! For then how could God judge the world? [7]But if through my falsehood God's truthfulness abounds to his glory, why am I still being condemned as a sinner? [8]And why not do evil that good may come?—as some people slanderously charge us with saying. Their condemnation is just.

9 What then? Are we Jews any better off? No, not at all; for I have already charged that all men, both Jews and Greeks, are under the power of sin, [10]as it is written:

"None is righteous, no, not one;
[11]no one understands, no one seeks for God.
[12]All have turned aside, together they have gone wrong;
no one does good, not even one."
[13]"Their throat is an open grave,
they use their tongues to deceive."
"The venom of asps is under their lips."
[14]"Their mouth is full of curses and bitterness."
[15]"Their feet are swift to shed blood,
[16]in their paths are ruin and misery,
[17]and the way of peace they do not know."
[18]"There is no fear of God before their eyes."

19 Now we know that whatever the law says it speaks to those who are under the law, so that every mouth may be stopped, and the whole world may be held accountable to God. [20]For no human being will be justified in his sight by works of the law since through the law comes knowledge of sin.

21 But now the righteousness of God has been manifested apart from law, although the law and the prophets bear witness to it, [22]the righteousness of God through faith in Jesus Christ for all who believe. For there is no distinction; [23]since all have sinned and fall short of the glory of God, [24]they are justified by his grace as a gift, through the redemption which is in Christ Jesus, [25]whom God put forward as an expiation by his blood, to be received by faith. This was to show God's righteousness, because in his divine forbearance he had passed over former sins; [26]it was to prove at the present time that he himself is righteous and that he justifies him who has faith in Jesus.

27 Then what becomes of our boasting? It is excluded. On what principle? On the principle of works? No, but on the principle of faith. [28]For we hold that a man is justified by faith apart from works of law. [29]Or is God the God of Jews only? Is he not the God of Gentiles also? Yes, of Gentiles also, [30]since God is one; and he will justify the circumcised on the ground of their faith and the uncircumcised because of their faith. [31]Do we then overthrow the law by this faith? By no means! On the contrary, we uphold the law.

CHAPTER 4

What then shall we say about Abraham, our forefather according to the flesh? [2]For if Abraham was justified by works, he has something to boast about, but not before God. [3]For what does the scripture say? "Abraham believed God, and it was reckoned to him as righteousness." [4]Now to one who works, his wages are not reckoned as a gift but as his due. [5]And to one who does not work but trusts him who justifies the ungodly, his faith is reckoned as righteousness. [6]So also David pronounces a blessing upon the man to whom God reckons righteousness apart from works:

[7]"Blessed are those whose iniquities are forgiven, and whose sins
are covered;
[8]blessed is the man against whom the Lord will not reckon his
sin."

9 Is this blessing pronounced only upon the circumcised, or also upon the uncircumcised? We say that faith was reckoned to Abraham as righteousness. [10]How then was it reckoned to him? Was it before or after he had been circumcised? It was not after, but before he was circumcised. [11]He received circumcision as a sign or seal of the righteousness which he had by faith while he was still uncircumcised. The purpose was to make

him the father of all who believe without being circumcised and who thus have righteousness reckoned to them, [12]and likewise the father of the circumcised who are not merely circumcised but who also follow the example of the faith which our father Abraham had before he was circumcised.

13 The promise to Abraham and his descendants, that they should inherit the world, did not come through the law but through the righteousness of faith. [14]If it is the adherents of the law who are to be the heirs, faith is null and the promise is void. [15]For the law brings wrath, but where there is no law there is no transgression.

16 That is why it depends on faith, in order that the promise may rest on grace and be guaranteed to all his descendants— not only to the adherents of the law but also to those who share the faith of Abraham, for he is the father of us all, [17]as it is written, "I have made you the father of many nations"—in the presence of the God in whom he believed, who gives life to the dead and calls into existence the things that do not exist.[18]In hope he believed against hope, that he should become the father of many nations; as he had been told, "So shall your descendants be." [19]He did not weaken in faith when he considered his own body, which was as good as dead because he was about a hundred years old, or when he considered the barrenness of Sarah's womb. [20]No distrust made him waver concerning the promise of God, but he grew strong in his faith as he gave glory to God, [21]fully convinced that God was able to do what he had promised. [22]That is why his faith was "reckoned to him as righteousness." [23]But the words, "it was reckoned to him," were written not for his sake alone, [24]but for ours also. It will be reckoned to us who believe in him that raised from the dead Jesus our Lord, [25]who was put to death for our trespasses and raised for our justification.

CHAPTER 5

Therefore, since we are justified by faith, we have peace with God through our Lord Jesus Christ. [2]Through him we have obtained access to this grace in which we stand, and we rejoice in our hope of sharing the glory of God. [3]More than that, we rejoice in our sufferings, knowing that suffering produces endurance, [4]and endurance produces character, and character produces hope, [5]and hope does not disappoint us, because God's love has been poured into our hearts through the Holy Spirit which has been given to us.

6 While we were yet helpless, at the right time Christ died for the ungodly. [7]Why, one will hardly die for a righteous man—though perhaps for a good man one will dare even to die. [8]But God shows his love for us in that while we were yet sinners Christ died for us. [9]Since, therefore, we are now justified by his blood, much more shall we be saved by him from the wrath of God. [10]For if while we were enemies we were reconciled to God by the death of his Son, much more, now that we are reconciled, shall we be saved by his life. [11]Not only so, but we also rejoice in God through our Lord Jesus Christ, through whom we have now received our reconciliation.

12 Therefore as sin came into the world through one man and death through sin, and so death spread to all men because all men sinned—[13]sin indeed was in the world before the law was given, but sin is not counted where there is no law. [14]Yet death reigned from Adam to Moses, even over those whose sins were not like the transgression of Adam, who was a type of the one who was to come.

15 But the free gift is not like the trespass. For if many died through one man's trespass, much more have the grace of God and the free gift in the grace of that one man Jesus Christ abounded for many. [16]And the free gift is not like the effect of that one man's sin. For the judgment following one trespass brought condemnation, but the free gift following many trespasses brings justification. [17]If, because of one man's trespass, death reigned through that one man, much more will those who receive the abundance of grace and the free gift of righteousness reign in life through the one man Jesus Christ.

18 Then as one man's trespass led to condemnation for all men, so one man's act of righteousness leads to acquittal and life for all men. [19]For as by one man's disobedience many were made sinners, so by one man's obedience many will be made righteous. [20]Law came in, to increase the trespass; but where sin increased, grace abounded all the more, [21]so that, as sin reigned in death, grace also might reign through righteousness to eternal life through Jesus Christ our Lord.

CHAPTER 6

What shall we say then? Are we to continue in sin that grace may abound? [2]By no means! How can we who died to sin still live in it? [3]Do you not know that all of us who have been baptized into Christ Jesus were baptized into his death? [4]We were buried therefore with him by baptism into death, so that as Christ was raised from the dead by the glory of the Father, we too might walk in newness of life.

5 For if we have been united with him in a death like his, we shall certainly be united with him in a resurrection like his. [6]We know that our old self was crucified with him so that the sinful body might be destroyed, and we might no longer be enslaved to sin. [7]For he who has died is freed from sin. [8]But if we have died with Christ, we believe that we shall also live with him. [9]For we know that Christ being raised from the dead will never die again; death no longer has dominion over him. [10]The death he died he died to sin, once for all, but the life he lives he lives to God. [11]So you also must consider yourselves dead to sin and alive to God in Christ Jesus.

12 Let not sin therefore reign in your mortal bodies, to make you obey their passions. [13]Do not yield your members to sin as instruments of wickedness, but yield yourselves to God as men who have been brought from death to life, and your members to God as instruments of righteousness. [14]For sin will have no dominion over you, since you are not under law but under grace.

15 What then? Are we to sin because we are not under law but under grace? By no means! [16]Do you not know that if you yield yourselves to any one as obedient slaves, you are slaves of the one whom you obey, either of sin, which leads to death, or of obedience, which leads to righteousness? [17]But thanks be to God, that you who were once slaves of sin have become obedient from the heart to the standard of teaching to which you were committed, [18]and, having been set free from sin, have become slaves of righteousness. [19]I am speaking in human terms, because of you natural limitations. For just as you once yielded your members to impurity and to greater and greater iniquity, so now yield your members to righteousness for sanctification.

20 When you were slaves of sin, you were free in regard to righteousness. [21]But then what return did you get from the things of which you are now ashamed? The end of those things is death. [22]But now that you have been set free from sin and have become slaves of God, the return you get is sanctification and its end, eternal life. [23]For the wages of sin is death, but the free gift of God is eternal life in Christ Jesus our Lord.

CHAPTER 7

Do you not know, brethren— for I am speaking to those who know the law— that the law is binding on a person only during his life? [2]Thus a married woman is bound by law to her husband as long as he lives; but if her husband dies she is discharged from the law concerning the husband. [3]Accordingly, she will be called an adulteress if she lives with another man while her husband is alive. But if her husband dies she is free from that law, and if she marries another man she is not an adulteress.

4 Likewise, my brethren, you have died to the law through the body of Christ, so that you may belong to another, to him who has been raised from the dead in order that we may bear fruit for God. [5]While we were living in the flesh, our sinful passions, aroused by the law, were at work in our members to bear fruit for death. [6]But now we are discharged from the law, dead to that which held us captive, so that we serve not under the old written code but in the new life of the Spirit.

7 What then shall we say? That the law is sin? By no means! Yet, if it had not been for the law, I should not have known sin. I should not have known what it is to covet if the law had not said, "You shall not covet." [8]But sin, finding opportunity in the commandment, wrought in me all kinds of covetousness. Apart from the law sin lies dead. [9]I was once alive apart from the law, but when the commandment came, sin revived and I died; [10]the very commandment which promised life proved to be death to me. [11]For sin, finding opportunity in the commandment, deceived me and by it killed me. [12]So the law is holy, and the commandment is holy and just and good.

13 Did that which is good, then, bring death to me? By no means! It was sin, working death in me through what is good, and in order that sin might be shown to be sin, and through the commandment might become sinful beyond measure. [14]We know that the law is spiritual; but I am carnal, sold under sin. [15]I do not understand my own actions. For I do not do what I want, but I do the very thing I hate. [16]Now if I do what I do not want, I agree that the law is good. [17]So then it is no longer I that do it, but sin which dwells within me. [18]For I know that nothing good dwells within me, that is, in my flesh. I can will what is right, but I cannot do it. [19]For I do not do the good I want, but the evil I do not want is what I do. [20]Now if I do what I do not want, it is no longer I that do it, but sin which dwells within me.

21 So I find it to be a law that when I want to do right, evil lies close at hand. [22]For I delight in the law of God, in my inmost self, [23]but I see in my members another law at war with the law of my mind and making me captive to the law of sin which dwells in my members. [24]Wretched man that I am! Who will deliver me from this body of death? [25]Thanks be to God through Jesus Christ our Lord! So then, I of myself serve the law of God with my mind, but with my flesh I serve the law of sin.

CHAPTER 8

There is therefore now no condemnation for those who are in Christ Jesus. [2]For the law of the Spirit of life in Christ Jesus has set me free from the law of sin and death. [3]For God has done what the law, weakened by the flesh, could not do: sending his own Son, in the likeness of sinful flesh and for sin, he condemned sin in the flesh, [4]in order that the just requirement of the law might be fulfilled in us, who walk not according to the flesh but according to the Spirit. [5]For those who live according to the flesh set their minds on the things of the flesh, but those who live according to the Spirit set their minds on the things of the Spirit. [6]To set the mind on the flesh is death, but to set the mind on the Spirit is life and peace. [7]For the mind that is set on the flesh is hostile to God; it does not submit to God's law, indeed it cannot; [8]and those who are in the flesh cannot please God.

9 But you are not in the flesh, you are in the Spirit, if the Spirit of God really dwells in you. Any one who does not have the spirit of Christ does not belong to him. [10]But if Christ is in you, although your bodies are dead because of sin, your spirits are alive because of righteousness. [11]If the Spirit of him who raised Jesus from the dead dwells in you, he who raised Christ Jesus from the dead will give life to your mortal bodies also through his Spirit which dwells in you.

12 So then, brethren, we are debtors, not to the flesh, to live according to the flesh—[13]for if you live according to the flesh you will die, but if by the Spirit you put to death the deeds of the body you will live. [14]For all who are led by the Spirit of God are sons of God. [15]For you did not receive the spirit of slavery to fall back into fear, but you have received the spirit of sonship. When we cry, "Abba! Father!" [16]it is the Spirit himself bearing witness with our spirit that we are children of God, [17]and if children, then heirs, heirs of God and fellow heirs with Christ, provided we suffer with him in order that we may also be glorified with him.

18 I consider that the sufferings of this present time are not worth comparing with the glory that is to be revealed to us. [19]For the creation waits with eager longing for the revealing of the sons of God; [20]for the creation was subjected to futility, not of its own will but by the will of him who subjected it in hope; [21]because the creation itself will be set free from its bondage to decay and obtain the glorious liberty of the children of God. [22]We know that the whole creation has been groaning in travail together until now; [23]and not only the creation, but we ourselves, who have the first fruits of the Spirit, groan inwardly as we wait for adoption as sons, the redemption of our bodies. [24]For in this hope we were saved.

Now hope that is seen is not hope. For who hopes for what he sees? [25]But if we hope for what we do not see, we wait for it with patience.

26 Likewise the Spirit helps us in our weakness; for we do not know how to pray as we ought, but the Spirit himself intercedes for us with sighs too deep for words. [27]And he who searches the hearts of men knows what is the mind of the Spirit, because the Spirit intercedes for the saints according to the will of God.

28 We know that in everything God works for good with those who love him, who are called according to his purpose. [29]For those whom he foreknew he also predestined to be conformed to the image of his Son, in order that he might be the first-born among many brethren. [30]And those whom he predestined he also called; and those whom he called he also justified; and those whom he justified he also glorified.

31 What then shall we say to this? If God is for us, who is against us? [32]He who did not spare his own Son but gave him up for us all, will he not also give us all things with him? [33]Who shall bring any charge against God's elect? It is God who justifies; [34]who is to condemn? Is it Christ Jesus, who died, yes, who was raised from the dead, who is at the right hand of God, who indeed intercedes for us? [35]Who shall separate us from the love of Christ? Shall tribulation, or distress, or persecution, or famine, or nakedness, or peril, or sword? [36]As it is written,

"For thy sake we are being killed all the day long;
we are regarded as sheep to be slaughtered."

[37]No, in all these things we are more than conquerors through him who loved us. [38]For I am sure that neither death, nor life, not angels, nor principalities, nor things present, nor things to come, nor powers, [39]nor height, nor depth, nor anything else in all creation, will be able to separate us from the love of God in Christ Jesus our Lord.

CHAPTER 9

I am speaking the truth in Christ, I am not lying; my conscience bears me witness in the Holy Spirit, [2]that I have great sorrow and unceasing anguish in my heart. [3]For I could wish that I myself were accursed and cut off from Christ for the sake of my brethren, my kinsmen by race. [4]They are Israelites, and to them belong the sonship, the glory, the covenants, the giving of the law, the worship, and the promises; [5]to them belong the patriarchs, and of their race, according to the flesh, is the Christ. God who is over all be blessed for ever. Amen.

6 But it is not as though the word of God had failed. For not all who are descended from Israel belong to Israel, [7]and not all are children of Abraham because they are his descendants; but "Through Isaac shall your descendants be named." [8]This means that it is not the children of the flesh who are the children of God, but the children of the promise are reckoned as descendants. [9]For this is what the promise said, "About this time I will return and Sarah shall have a son." [10]And not only so, but also when Rebecca had conceived children by one man, our forefather Isaac, [11]though they were not yet born and had done nothing either good or bad, in order that God's purpose of election might continue, not because of works but because of his call, [12]she was told, "The elder will serve the younger." [13]As it is written, "Jacob I loved, but Esau I hated."

14 What shall we say then? Is there injustice on God's part? By no means! [15]For he says to Moses, "I will have mercy on whom I have mercy, and I will have compassion on whom I have compassion." [16]So it depends not upon man's will or exertion, but upon God's mercy. [17]For the scripture says to Pharaoh, "I have raised you up for the very purpose of showing my power in you, so that my name may be proclaimed in all the earth." [18]So then he has mercy upon whomever he wills, and he hardens the heart of whomever he wills.

19 You will say to me then, "Why does he still find fault? For who can resist his will?" [20]But, who are you, a man, to answer back to God? Will what is molded say to its molder, "Why have you made me thus?" [21]Has the potter no right over the clay, to make out of the same lump one vessel for beauty and another for menial use? [22]What if God, desiring to show his wrath and to make known his power, has endured with much patience the vessels of wrath made for destruction, [23]in order to make known the riches of his glory for the vessels of mercy, which he has prepared beforehand for glory, [24]even us whom he has called, not from the Jews only but also from the Gentiles? [25]As indeed he says in Hosea,

"Those who were not my people
I will call 'my people'
and her who was not beloved
I will call 'my beloved.'"

[26]"And in the very place where it was said to them,
'You are not my people,'
they will be called 'sons of the living God.'"

27 And Isaiah cries out concerning Israel: "Though the number of the sons of Israel be as the sand of the sea, only a remnant of them will be

saved; [28]for the Lord will execute his sentence upon the earth with rigor and dispatch." [29]And as Isaiah predicted,

"If the Lord of hosts had not left us children,
we would have fared like Sodom and been made like Gomorrah."

30 What shall we say, then? That Gentiles who did not pursue righteousness have attained it, that is, righteousness through faith; [31]but that Israel who pursued the righteousness which is based on law did not succeed in fulfulling that law. [32]Why? Because they did not pursue it through faith, but as if it were based on works. They have stumbled over the stumbling stone, [33]as it is written,

"Behold I am laying in Zion a stone that will make men stumble,
a rock that will make them fall;
and he who believes in him will not be put to shame."

CHAPTER 10

Brethren, my heart's desire and prayer to God for them is that they may be saved. [2]I bear them witness that they have a zeal for God, but it is not enlightened. [3]For, being ignorant of the righteousness that comes from God, and seeking to establish their own, they did not submit to God's righteousness. [4]For Christ is the end of the law, that every one who has faith may be justified.

5 Moses writes that the man who practices the righteousness which is based on the law shall live by it. [6]But the righteousness based on faith says, Do not say in your heart, "Who will ascend into heaven?" (that is, to bring Christ down) [7]or "Who will descend into the abyss?" (that is, to bring Christ up from the dead). [8]But what does it say? The word is near you, on your lips and in your heart (that is, the word of faith which we preach); [9]because, if you confess with your lips that Jesus is Lord and believe in your heart that God raised him from the dead, you will be saved. [10]For man believes with his heart and so is justified, and he confesses with his lips and so is saved. [11]The scripture says, "No one who believes in him will be put to shame." [12]For there is no distinction between Jew and Greek; the same Lord is Lord of all and bestows his riches upon all who call upon him. [13]For, "every one who calls upon the name of the Lord will be saved."

14 But how are men to call upon him in whom they have not believed? And how are they to believe in him of whom they have never heard? And how are they to hear without a preacher? [15]And how can men preach unless they are sent? As it is written, "How beautiful are the feet of those

who preach good news!" [16]But they have not all heeded the gospel; for Isaiah says, "Lord, who has believed what he has heard from us?" [17]So faith comes from what is heard, and what is heard comes by the preaching of Christ.

18 But I ask, have they not heard? Indeed they have; for
"Their voice has gone out to all the earth,
and their words to the ends of the world."

[19]Again I ask, did Israel not understand? First Moses says,
"I will make you jealous of those who are not a nation;
with a foolish nation I will make you angry."

[20]Then Isaiah is so bold as to say,
"I have been found by those who did not seek me;
I have shown myself to those who did not ask for me."

[21]But of Israel he says, "All day long I have held out my hands to a disobedient and contrary people."

CHAPTER 11

I ask, then, has God rejected his people? By no means! I myself am an Israelite, a descendant of Abraham, a member of the tribe of Benjamin. [2]God has not rejected his people whom he foreknew. Do you not know what the scripture says of Elijah, how he pleads with God against Israel? [3]"Lord, they have killed thy prophets, they have demolished thy altars, and I alone am left, and they seek my life." [4]But what is God's reply to him? "I have kept for myself seven thousand men who have not bowed the knee to Baal." [5]So too at the present time there is a remnant, chosen by grace. [6]But if it is by grace, it is no longer on the basis of works; otherwise grace would no longer be grace.

7 What then? Israel failed to obtain what it sought. The elect obtained it, but the rest were hardened, [8]as it is written,
"God gave them a spirit of stupor,
eyes that should not see and ears that should not hear,
down to this very day."

[9]And David says,
"Let their feast become a snare and a trap,
a pitfall and a retribution for them;
[10]let their eyes be darkened so that they cannot see,
and bend their backs for ever."

11 So I ask, have they stumbled so as to fall? By no means! But through their trespass salvation has come to the Gentiles, so as to make Israel

jealous. [12]Now if their trespass means riches for the world, and if their failure means riches for the Gentiles, how much more will their full inclusion mean!

13 Now I am speaking to you Gentiles. Inasmuch then as I am an apostle to the Gentiles, I magnify my ministry [14]in order to make my fellow Jews jealous, and thus save some of them. [15]For if their rejection means the reconciliation of the world, what will their acceptance mean but life from the dead? [16]If the dough offered as first fruits is holy, so is the whole lump; and if the root is holy, so are the branches.

17 But if some of the branches were broken off, and you, a wild olive shoot, were grafted in their place to share the richness of the olive tree, [18]do not boast over the branches. If you do boast, remember it is not you that support the root, but the root that supports you. [19]You will say, "Branches were broken off so that I might be grafted in." [20]That is true. They were broken off because of their unbelief, but you stand fast only through faith. So do not become proud, but stand in awe. [21]For if God did not spare the natural branches, neither will he spare you. [22]Note then the kindness and the severity of God: severity toward those who have fallen, but God's kindness to you, provided you continue in his kindness; otherwise you too will be cut off. [23]And even the others, if they do not persist in their unbelief, will be grafted in, for God has the power to graft them in again. [24]For if you have been cut from what is by nature a wild olive tree, and grafted, contrary to nature, into a cultivated olive tree, how much more will these natural branches be grafted back into their own olive tree.

25 Lest you be wise in your own conceits, I want you to understand this mystery, brethren: a hardening has come upon part of Israel, until the full number of the Gentiles comes in, [26]and so all Israel will be saved; as it is written,

"The Deliverer will come from Zion,
he will banish ungodliness from Jacob";
[27]"and this will be my covenant with them
when I take away their sins."

[28]As regards the gospel they are enemies of God, for your sake; but as regards election they are beloved for the sake of their forefathers. [29]For the gifts and the call of God are irrevocable. [30]Just as you were once disobedient to God but now have received mercy because of their disobedience, [31]so they have now been disobedient in order that by the mercy shown to you they also may receive mercy. [32]For God has consigned all men to disobedience, that he may have mercy upon all.

33 O the depth of the riches and wisdom and knowledge of God! How unsearchable are his judgments and how inscrutable his ways!
[34]"For who has known the mind of the Lord,
or who has been his counselor?"
[35]"Or who has given a gift to him
that he might be repaid?"
[36]For from him and through him and to him are all things. To him be glory forever. Amen.

CHAPTER 12

I appeal to you therefore, brethren, by the mercies of God, to present your bodies as a living sacrifice, holy and acceptable to God, which is your spiritual worship. [2]Do not be conformed to this world but be transformed by the renewal of your mind, that you may prove what is the will of God, what is good and acceptable and perfect.

3 For by the grace given to me I bid everyone among you not to think of himself more highly than he ought to think, but to think with sober judgment, each according to the measure of faith which God has assigned him. [4]For as in one body we have many members, and all the members do not have the same function, [5]so we, though many, are one body in Christ, and individually members one of another. [6]Having gifts that differ according to the grace given to us, let us use them: if prophecy, in proportion to our faith;[7]if service, in our serving; he who teaches, in his teaching; [8]he who exhorts, in his exhortation; he who contributes, in liberality; he who gives aid, with zeal; he who does acts of mercy, with cheerfulness.

9 Let love be genuine; hate what is evil, hold fast to what is good; [10]love one another with brotherly affection; outdo one another in showing honor. [11]Never flag in zeal, be aglow with the Spirit, serve the Lord. [12]Rejoice in your hope, be patient in tribulation, be constant in prayer. [13]Contribute to the needs of the saints, practice hospitality.

14 Bless those who persecute you; bless and do not curse them. [15]Rejoice with those who rejoice, weep with those who weep. [16]Live in harmony with one another; do not be haughty, but associate with the lowly; never be conceited. [17]Repay no one evil for evil, but take thought for what is noble in the sight of all. [18]If possible, so far as it depends upon you, live peaceably with all. [19]Beloved, never avenge yourselves, but leave it to the wrath of God; for it is written, "Vengeance is mine, I will repay, says the Lord." [20]No, "if your enemy is hungry, feed him; if he is thirsty,

give him drink; for by so doing you will heap burning coals upon his head." [21]Do not be overcome by evil, but overcome evil with good.

CHAPTER 13

Let every person be subject to the governing authorities. For there is no authority except from God, and those that exist have been instituted by God. [2]Therefore he who resists the authorities resists what God has appointed, and those who resist will incur judgment. [3]For rulers are not a terror to good conduct, but to bad. Would you have no fear of him who is in authority? Then do what is good, and you will receive his approval, [4]for he is God's servant for your good. But if you do wrong, be afraid, for he does not bear the sword in vain; he is the servant of God to execute his wrath on the wrongdoer. [5]Therefore one must be subject, not only to avoid God's wrath but also for the sake of conscience. [6]For the same reason you also pay taxes, for the authorities are ministers of God, attending to this very thing. [7]Pay all of them their dues, taxes to whom taxes are due, revenue to whom revenue is due, respect to whom respect is due, honor to whom honor is due.

8 Owe no one anything, except to love one another; for he who loves his neighbor has fulfilled the law. [9]The commandments, "You shall not commit adultery, You shall not kill, You shall not steal, You shall not covet," and any other commandment are summed up in this sentence, "You shall love your neighbor as yourself." [10]Love does no wrong to a neighbor; therefore love is the fulfilling of the law.

11 Besides this you know what hour it is, how it is full time now for you to wake from sleep. For salvation is nearer to us now than when we first believed; [12]the night is far gone, the day is at hand. Let us then cast off the works of darkness and put on the armor of light; [13]let us conduct ourselves becomingly as in the day, not in reveling and drunkenness, not in debauchery and licentiousness, not in quarreling and jealousy. [14]But put on the Lord Jesus Christ, and make no provision for the flesh, to gratify its desires.

CHAPTER 14

As for the man who is weak in faith, welcome him, but not for disputes over opinions. [2]One believes he may eat anything, while the weak man eats only vegetables. [3]Let not him who eats despise him who abstains, and let not him who abstains pass judgment on him who eats; for God has welcomed him. [4]Who are you to pass judgment on the servant of another? It is before his own master that he stands or falls. And he will be upheld, for the Master is able to make him stand.

5 One man esteems one day as better than another, while another man esteems all days alike. Let every one be fully convinced in his own mind. [6]He who observes the day, observes it in honor of the Lord. He also who eats, eats in honor of the Lord, since he gives thanks to God; while he who abstains, abstains in honor of the Lord and gives thanks to God. [7]None of us lives to himself, and none of us dies to himself. [8]If we live, we live to the Lord, and if we die, we die to the Lord; so then, whether we live or whether we die, we are the Lord's. [9]For to this end Christ died and lived again, that he might be Lord both of the dead and of the living.

10 Why do you pass judgment on your brother? Or you, why do you despise your brother? For we shall all stand before the judgment seat of God; [11]for it is written,

"As I live, says the Lord, every knee shall bow to me,
and every tongue shall give praise to God."

[12]So each of us shall give account of himself to God.

13 Then let us no more pass judgment on one another, but rather decide never to put a stumbling-block or hindrance in the way of a brother. [14]I know and am persuaded in the Lord Jesus that nothing is unclean in itself; but it is unclean for anyone who thinks it unclean. [15]If your brother is being injured by what you eat, you are no longer walking in love. Do not let what you eat cause the ruin of one for whom Christ died. [16]So do not let what is good to you be spoken of as evil. [17]For the kingdom of God does not mean food and drink but righteousness and peace and joy in the Holy Spirit; [18]he who thus serves Christ is acceptable to God and approved by men. [19]Let us then pursue what makes for peace and for mutual upbuilding. [20]Do not, for the sake of food, destroy the work of God. Everything is indeed clean, but it is wrong for any one to make others fall by what he eats; [21]it is right not to eat meat or drink wine or do anything that makes your brother stumble. [22]The faith that you have, keep between yourself and God; happy is he who has no reason to judge himself for what he approves. [23]But he who has doubts is condemned, if he eats, because he does not act from faith; for whatever does not proceed from faith is sin.

CHAPTER 15

We who are strong ought to bear with the failings of the weak, and not to please ourselves; [2]let each of us please his neighbor for his good, to edify him. [3]For Christ did not please himself; but, as it is written, "The reproaches of those who reproached thee fell on me." [4]For whatever was written in former days was written for our instruction, that by steadfastness and by the encouragement of the scriptures we might have hope. [5]May the God of steadfastness and encouragement grant you to live in such harmony with one another, in accord with Christ Jesus, [6]that together you may with one voice glorify the God and Father of our Lord Jesus Christ.

7 Welcome one another, therefore, as Christ has welcomed you, for the glory of God. [8]For I tell you that Christ became a servant to the circumcised to show God's truthfulness, in order to confirm the promises given to the patriarchs, [9]and in order that the Gentiles might glorify God for his mercy. As it is written,

"Therefore I will praise thee among the Gentiles,
and sing to thy name";

[10]and again it is said,

"Rejoice, O Gentiles, with his people";

[11]and again,

"Praise the Lord, all Gentiles,
and let all the peoples praise him";

[12]and further Isaiah says,

"The root of Jesse shall come,
he who rises to rule the Gentiles;
in him shall the Gentiles hope."

[13]May the God of hope fill you with all joy and peace in believing, so that by the power of the Holy Spirit you may abound in hope.

14 I myself am satisfied about you, my brethren, that you yourselves are full of goodness, filled with all knowledge, and able to instruct one another. [15]But on some points I have written to you very boldly by way of reminder, because of the grace given me by God [16]to be a minister of Christ Jesus to the Gentiles in the priestly service of the gospel of God, so that the offering of the Gentiles may be acceptable, sanctified by the Holy Spirit. [17]In Christ Jesus, then, I have reason to be proud of my work for God. [18]For I will not venture to speak of anything except what Christ has wrought through me to win obedience from the Gentiles, by word and deed, [19]by the power of signs and wonders by the power of the Holy Spirit, so that from Jerusalem and as far round as Illyricum I have fully preached the gospel of Christ, [20]thus making it my ambition to preach the gospel, not where Christ has already been named, lest I build on another man's foundation, [21]but as it is written,

"They shall see who have never been told of him,
and they shall understand who have never heard of him."

22 This is the reason why I have so often been hindered from coming to you. [23]But now, since I no longer have any room for work in these regions, and since I have longed for many years to come to you, [24]I hope to see you in passing as I go to Spain, and to be sped on my journey there by you, once I have enjoyed your company for a little. [25]At present, however, I am going to Jerusalem with aid for the saints. [26]For Macedonia and Achaia have been pleased to make some contribution for the poor among the saints at Jerusalem; [27]they were pleased to do it, and indeed they are in debt to them, for if the Gentiles have come to share in their spiritual blessings they ought also to be of service to them in material blessings. [28]When therefore I have completed this, and have delivered to them what has been raised, I shall go on by way of you to Spain; [29]and I know that when I come to you I shall come in the fulness of the blessing of Christ.

30 I appeal to you, brethren, by our Lord Jesus Christ and by the love of the Spirit, to strive together with me in your prayers to God on my behalf, [31]that I may be delivered from the unbelievers in Judea, and that my service for Jerusalem may be acceptable to the saints, [32]so that by God's will I may come to you with joy and be refreshed in your company. [33]The God of peace be with you all. Amen.

CHAPTER 16

I commend to you our sister Phoebe, a deaconess of the church at Cenchreae, [2]that you may receive her in the Lord as befits the saints, and help her in whatever she may require from you, for she has been a helper of many and of myself as well.

3 Greet Prisca and Aquila, my fellow workers in Christ Jesus, [4]who risked their necks for my life, to whom not only I but also all the churches of the Gentiles give thanks; [5]greet also the church in their house. Greet my beloved Epaenetus, who was the first convert in Asia for Christ. [6]Greet Mary, who has worked hard among you. [7]Greet Andronicus and Junias, my kinsmen and my fellow prisoners; they are men of note among the apostles, and they were in Christ before me. [8]Greet Ampliatus, my beloved in the Lord. [9]Greet Urbanus, our fellow worker in Christ, and my beloved Stachys. [10]Greet Apelles, who is approved in Christ. Greet those who belong to the family of Aristobulus. [11]Greet my kinsman Herodion. Greet

those in the Lord who belong to the family of Narcissus. [12]Greet those workers in the Lord, Tryphaena and Tryphosa. Greet the beloved Persis, who has worked hard in the Lord. [13]Greet Rufus, eminent in the Lord, also his mother and mine. [14]Greet Asyncritus, Phlegon, Hermes, Patrobas, Hermas, and the brethren who are with them. [15]Greet Philologus, Julia, Nereus and his sister, and Olympas, and all the saints who are with them. [16]Greet one another with a holy kiss. All the churches of Christ greet you.

17 I appeal to you, brethren, to take note of those who create dissensions and difficulties, in opposition to the doctrine which you have been taught; avoid them. [18]For such persons do not serve our Lord Christ, but their own appetites, and by fair and flattering words they deceive the hearts of the simple-minded. [19]For while your obedience is known to all, so that I rejoice over you, I would have you wise as to what is good and guileless as to what is evil; [20]then the God of peace will soon crush Satan under your feet. The grace of Lord Jesus Christ be with you.

21 Timothy, my fellow worker, greets you; so do Lucius and Jason and Sosipater, my kinsmen.

22 I Tertius, the writer of this letter, greet you in the Lord.

23 Gaius, who is host to me and to the whole church, greets you. Erastus, the city treasurer, and our brother Quartus, greet you.

25 Now to him who is able to strengthen you according to my gospel and the preaching of Jesus Christ, according to the revelation of the mystery which was kept secret for long ages [26]but is now disclosed and through the prophetic writings is made known to all nations, according to the command of the eternal God, to bring about obedience to the faith—[27]to the only wise God be glory for evermore through Jesus Christ! Amen.

Notes

1. T. W. Manson, "St. Paul's Letter to the Romans—and Others," in *Studies in the Gospels and Epistles*, ed. M. Black (Manchester: Manchester University Press, 1962), 225–41. Reprinted in *The Romans Debate* (Minneapolis: Augsburg Publishing House, 1977; revised and expanded edition, Peabody, Mass.: Hendrickson, 1991); this volume is a good companion to the study of Romans.

2. Wolfgang Wiefel, "The Jewish Community in Ancient Rome and the Origins of Roman Christianity," in *The Romans Debate*, 100–119; German original in *Judaica* 26 (1970) 65–88.

3. Joachim Jeremias, *The Prayers of Jesus* (Fortress Press, 1978); but see J. Fitzmyer, "Abba and Jesus' Relation to God," in *À Cause d'Évangile*, Lectio Divina 123 (1988), and recent articles by Mary Rose d'Angelo in the *Journal of Biblical Literature* 111 (1992) 611–30 and the *Harvard Theological Review* 85 (1992) 149–74.

4. Paul Schubert, *Form and Function of the Pauline Thanksgiving*, Beihefte zur *Zeitschrift für die neutestamentliche Wissenschaft* 20 (1939).

5. Cicero, *De Re Publica* 1.58.

6. S. K. Williams, "The Righteousness of God in Romans," *Journal of Biblical Literature* 99 (1980) 241–90. Morna Hooker has sorted out the problem in a nuanced and convincing manner in her Presidential Address to the Studiorum Novi Testamenti Societas: "Pistis Christou," *New Testament Studies* 35 (1989), 321–42.

7. S. Lyonnet in *Verbum Domini* 40 (1962) 163–83. See also his *La Bible de Jérusalem Commentary*, 2d ed., 1959.

8. C. S. Song's chapter "Many Peoples, Many Languages," in his *The Compassionate God* (1982), 21–40.

9. C. E. B. Cranfield, *Romans*, vol. 2, International Critical Commentary (1979), 613–16.

10. Already in my *Paul among Jews and Gentiles* (Fortress, 1976) I had the opportunity to discuss Käsemann's understanding of Paul in general and of Romans in particular. His *Commentary on Romans* has been available in English translation since 1980 (Grand Rapids: Eerdmans). His conviction that the future of Protestantism is at stake in the kind of discussions that we have been engaged in is expressed most forcefully in his extensive attack on my old piece on "Paul and the Introspective Conscience of the West" (*Paul among Jews and Gentiles*, 78–96). That discussion appeared in his *Perspectives on Paul* (Fortress, 1971), 59–78. My attempt at an answer is found in *Paul among Jews and Gentiles*, 129–33.

11. The fact that I read "conviction" and Käsemann reads "faith" illustrates quite clearly our respective styles of exegesis. For me the isses are concrete and specific. My method is often minimalist. Käsemann is a theological maximalist for whom the Pauline keywords have in them all the depth that later traditions found in them. That same difference shows not least in our understandings of the verse that constitutes the very center of Käsemann's interpretation, and where "the decisive question of the doctrine of justification, the epistle, and Paul's theology as a whole" (*Romans*, 111) is in focus, i.e. Romans 4:5. As we have seen, this is where Abraham exemplifies those who are justified as they "believe in the One who justifies the ungodly." According to Käsemann, Paul here "defines the nature of faith at the deepest level by the justification of the ungodly" (same page). For me Paul's point is less deep and more to the point in his specific argument. Abraham was "justified" while still a Gentile sinner—to use the phrase from Galatians (2:15; cf. the parallel reasoning in Gal. 3:6–9). The issue at hand in Romans is the justification of Paul's Gentile converts, not of sinners in general. There I rest the argument.

LaVergne, TN USA
30 December 2010

210544LV00004B/17/P